Christmas

2

Coloring Book

Adult Colouring Books

Aryla Publishing 2019

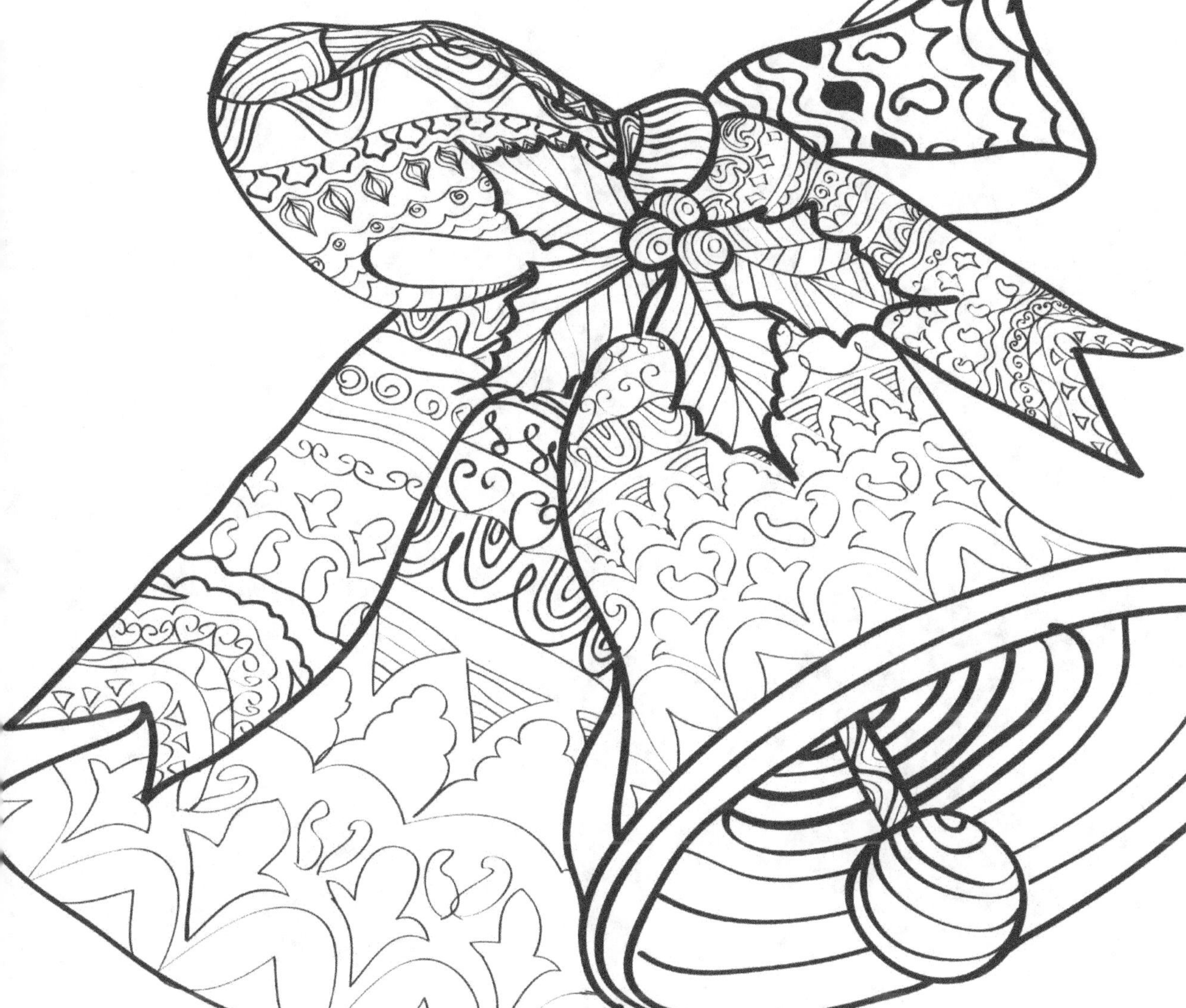

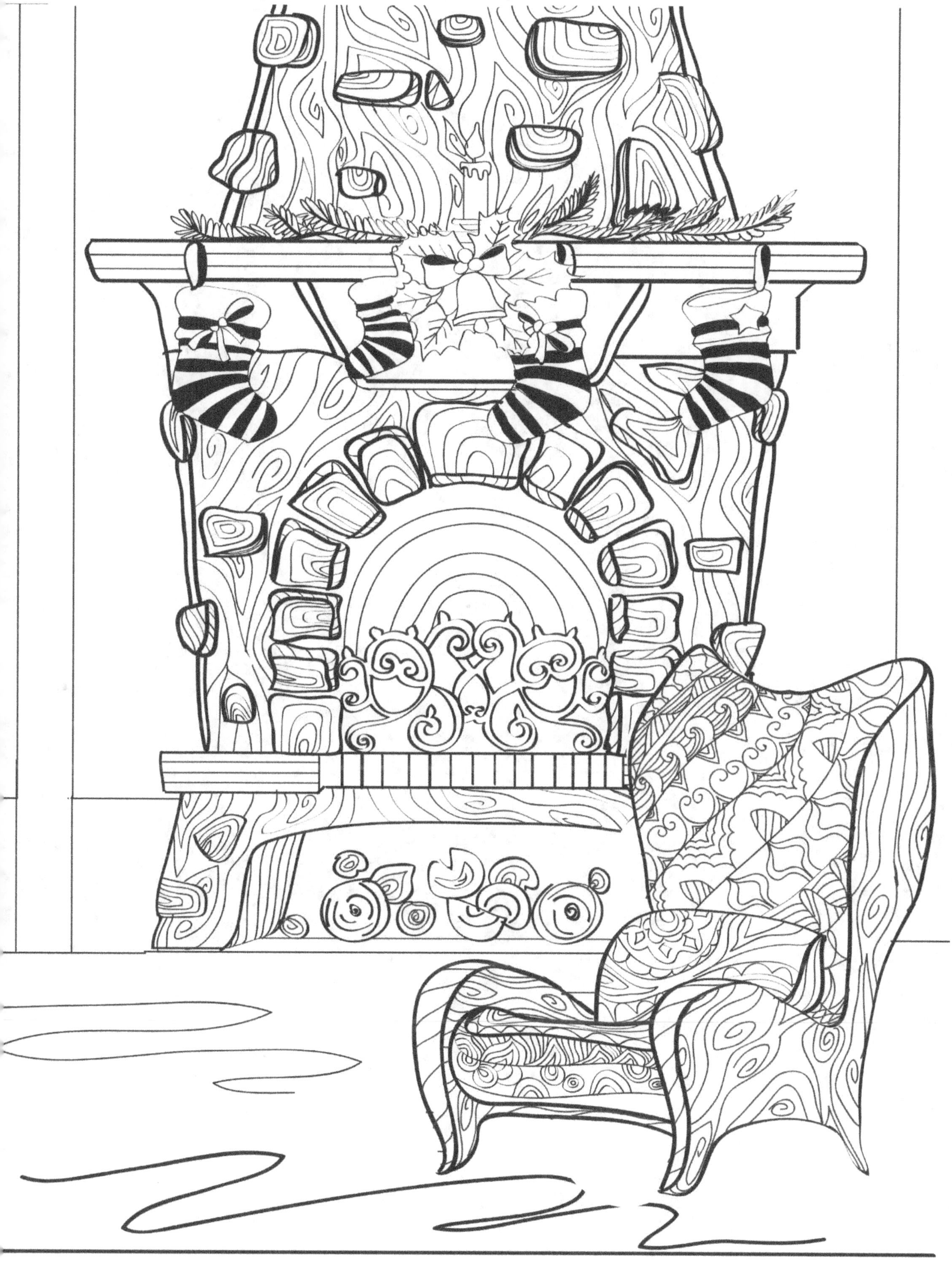

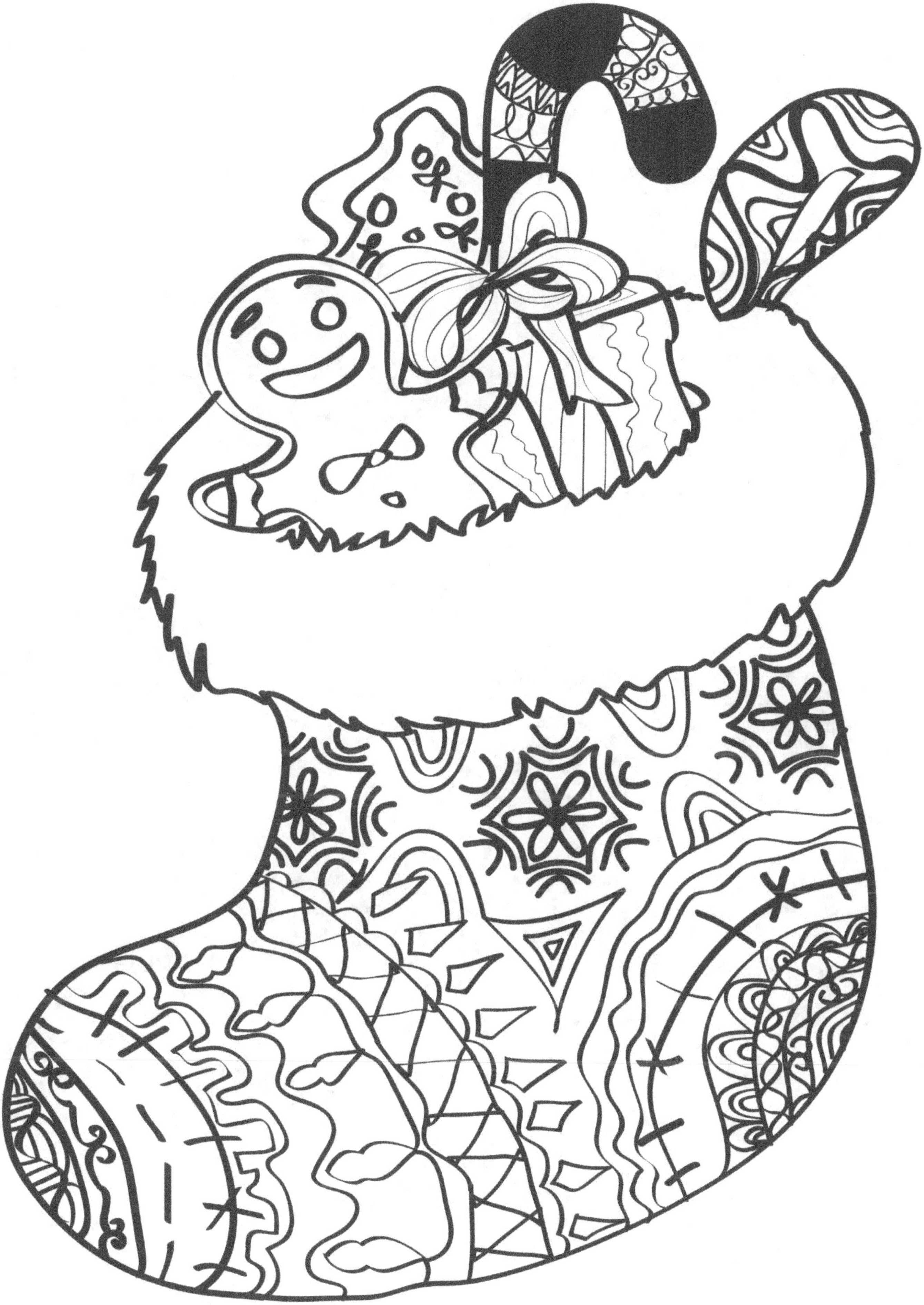

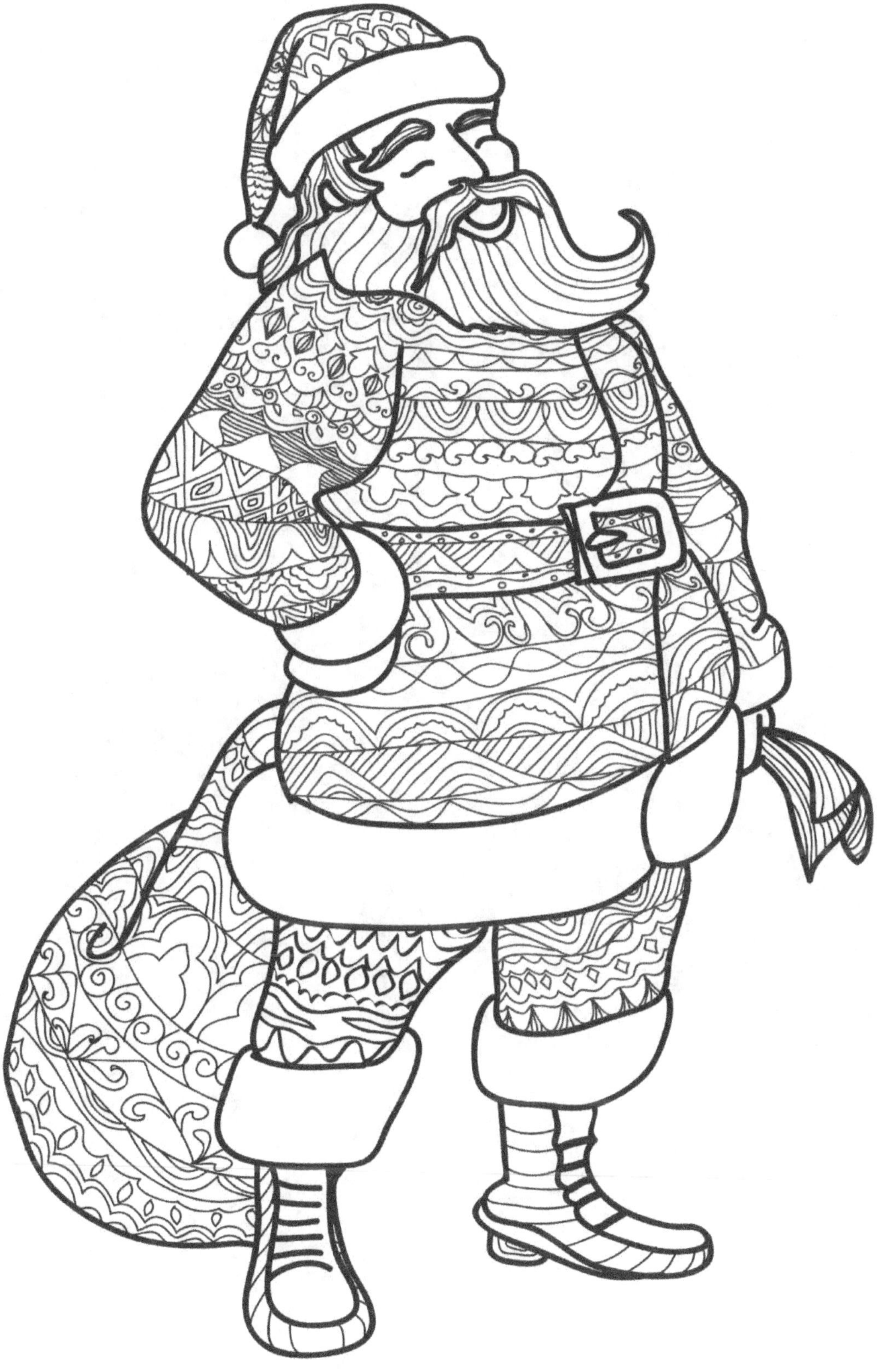

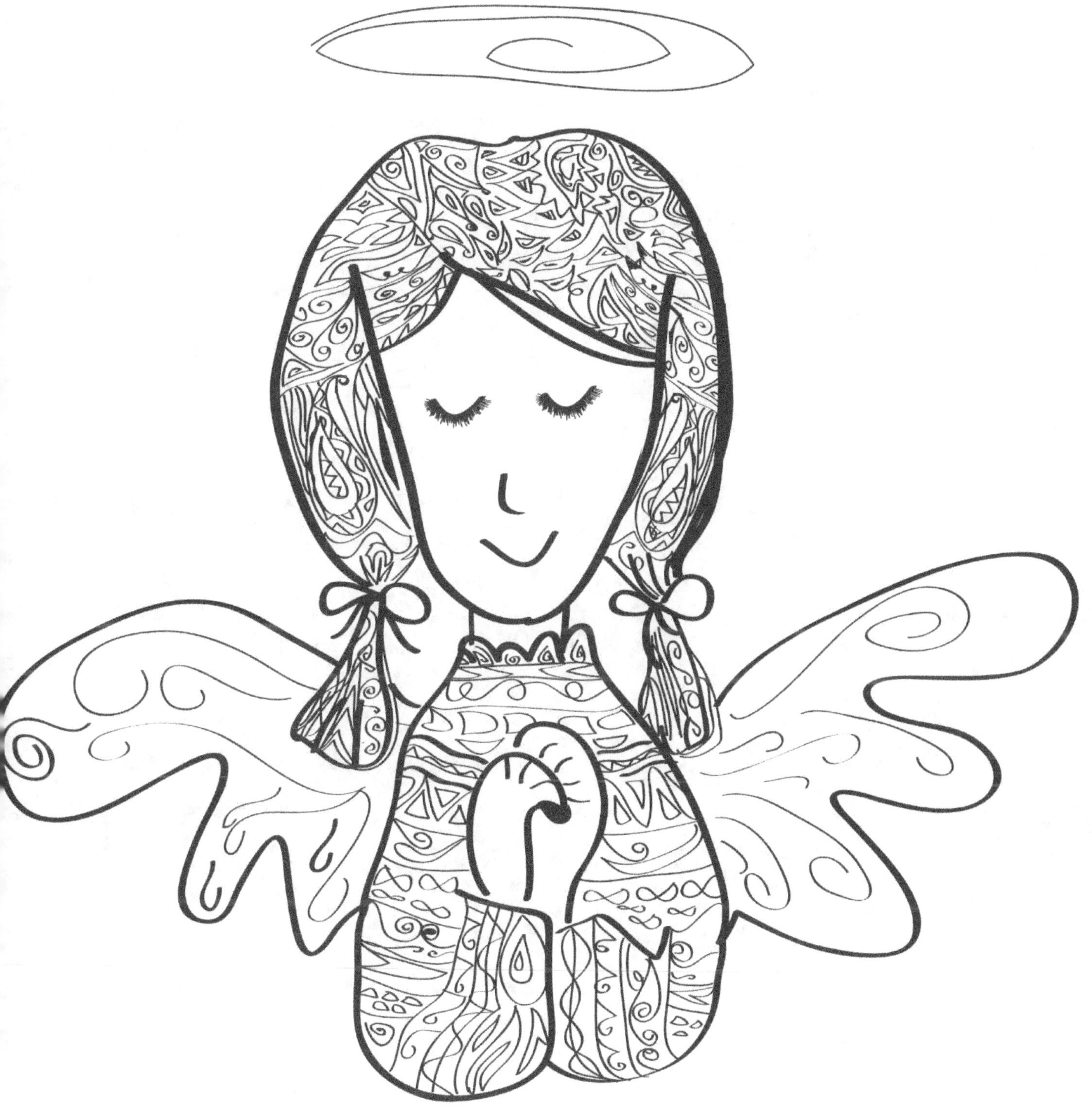

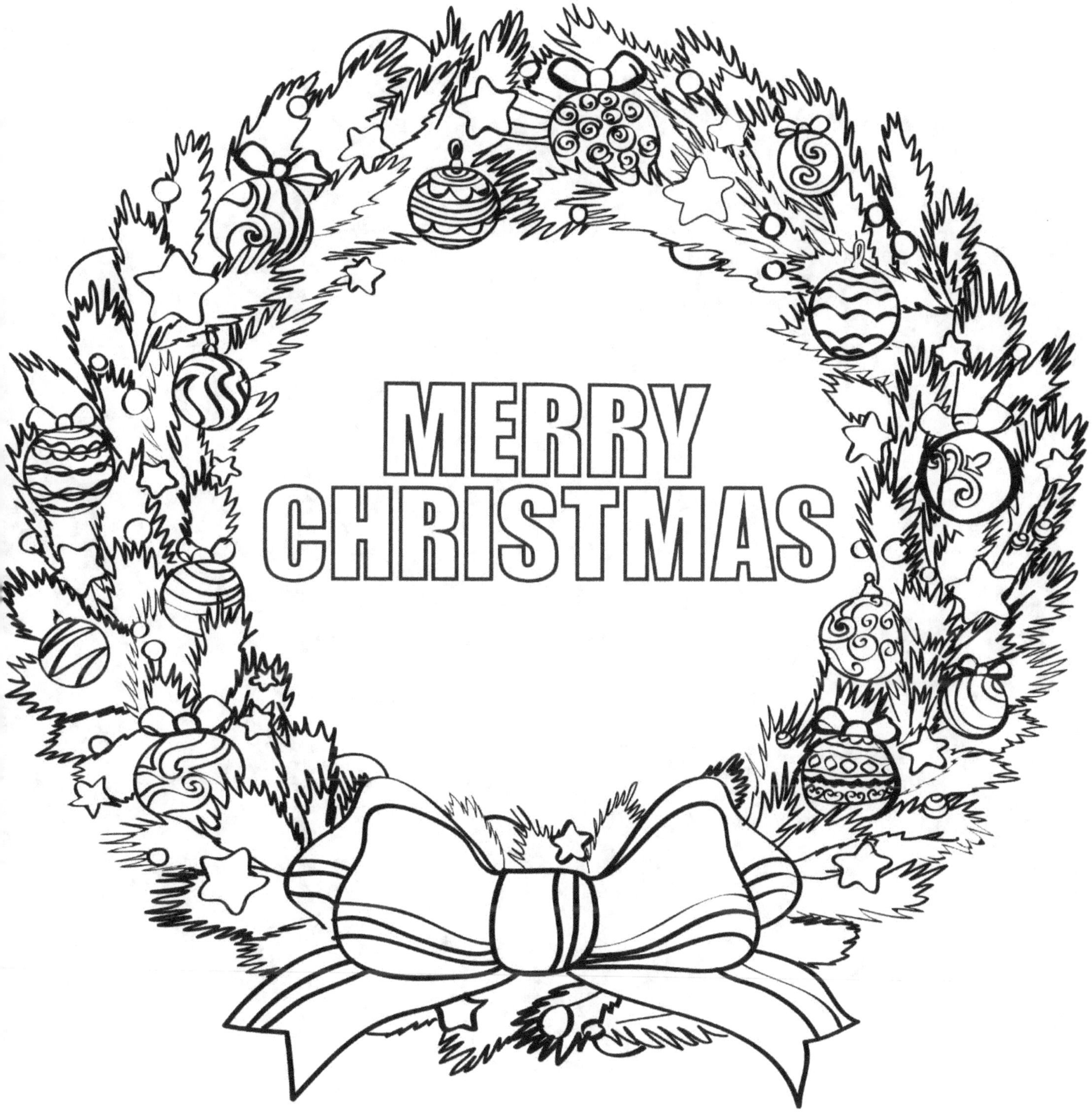
MERRY
CHRISTMAS

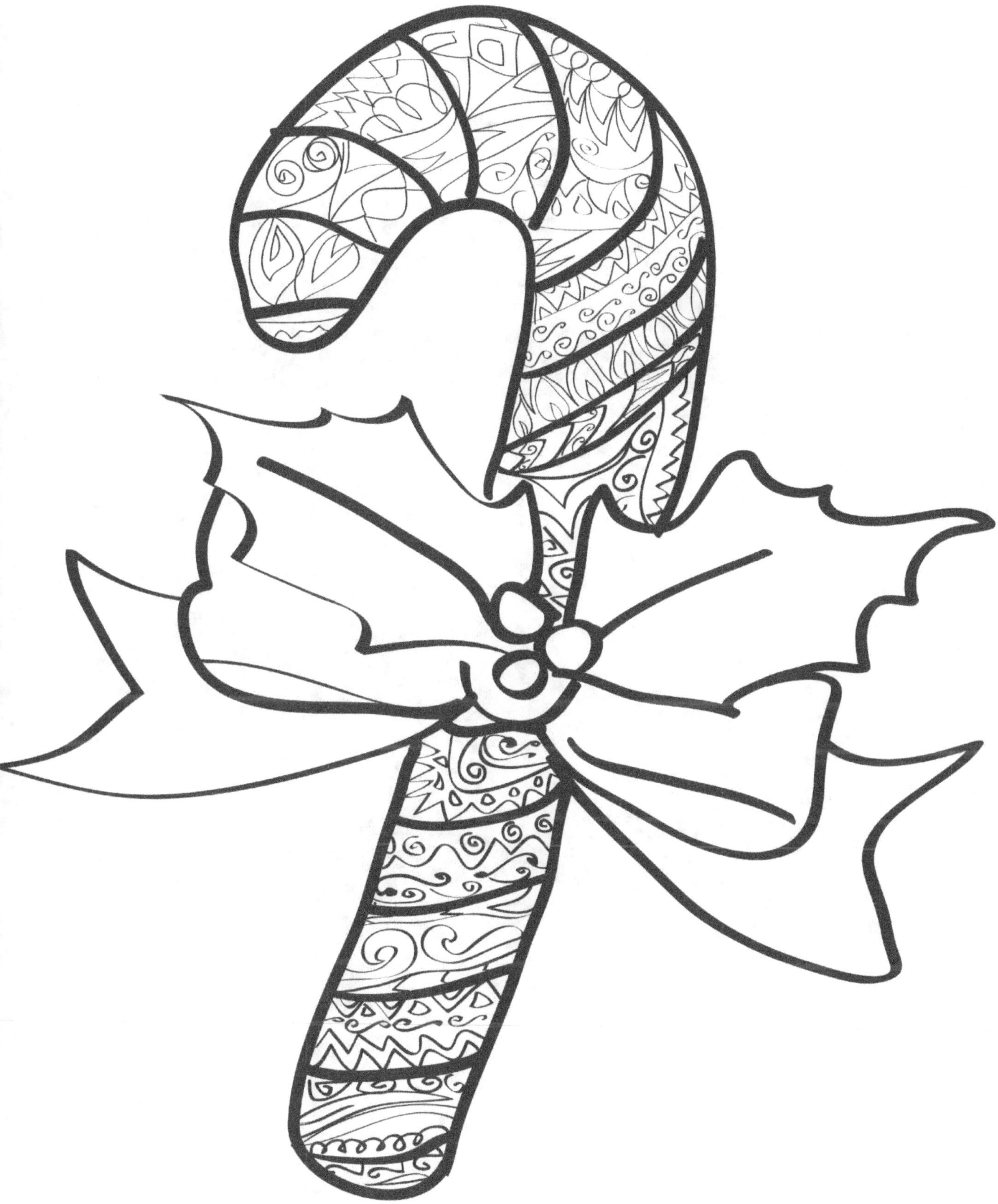

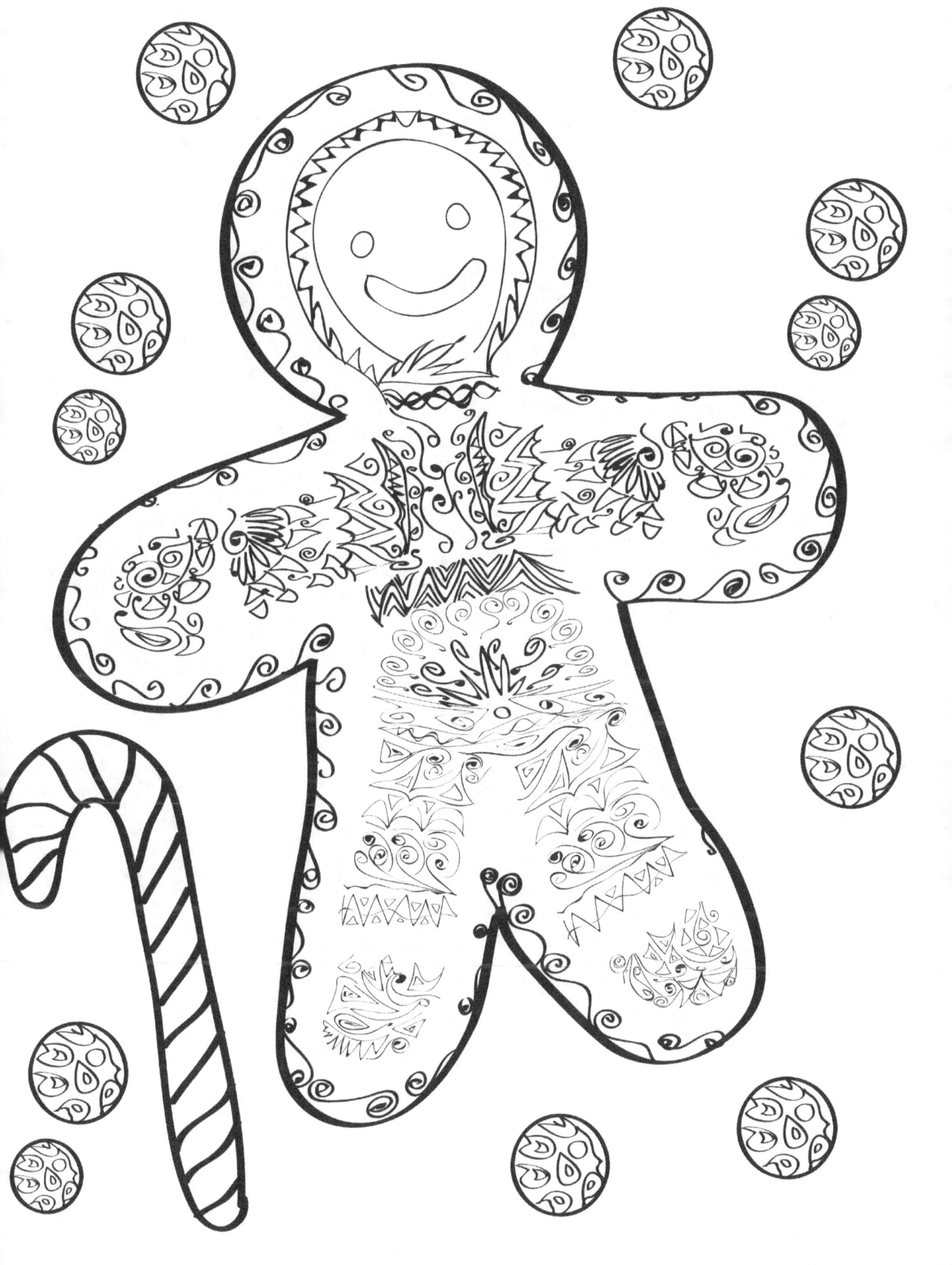

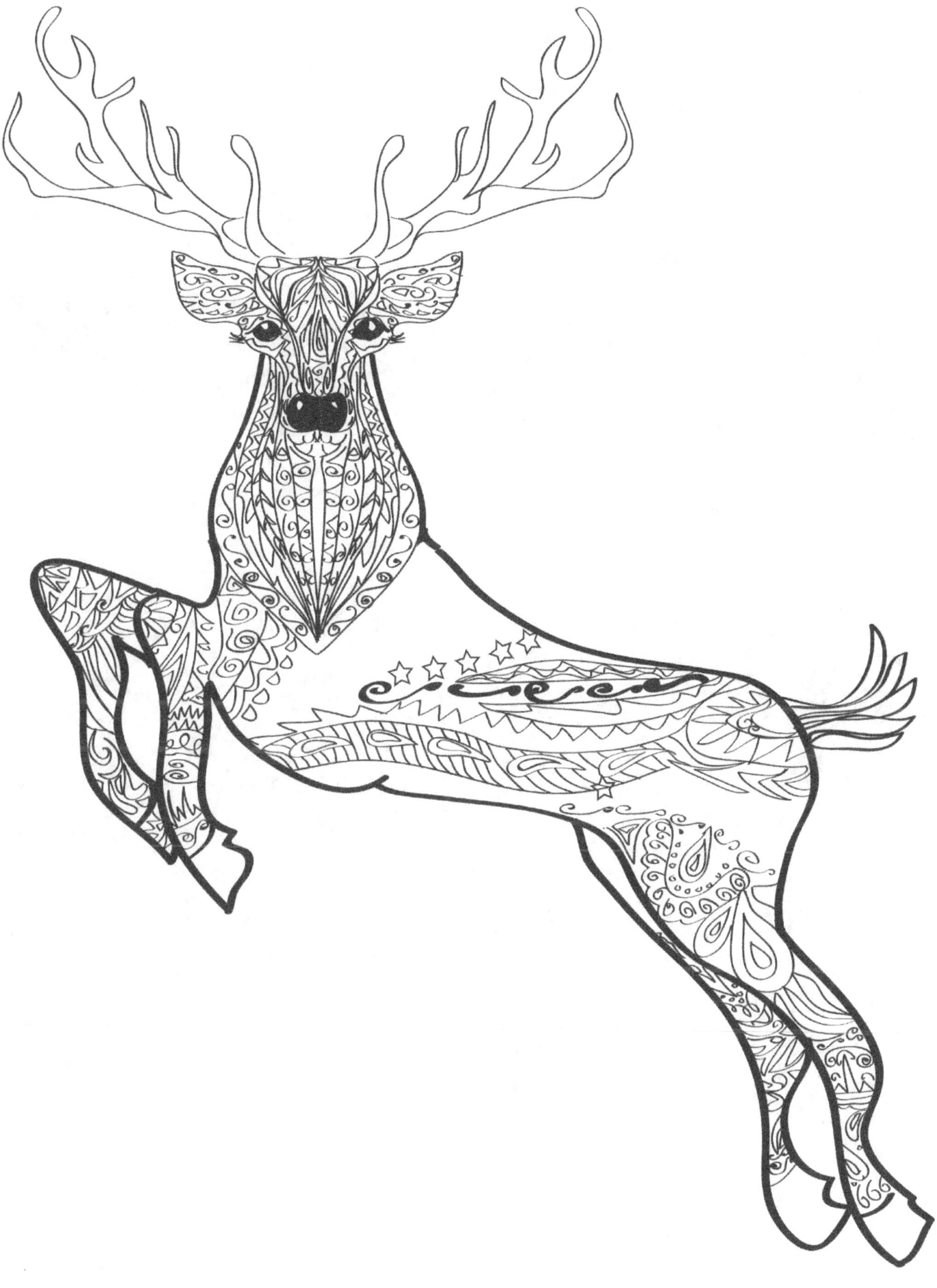

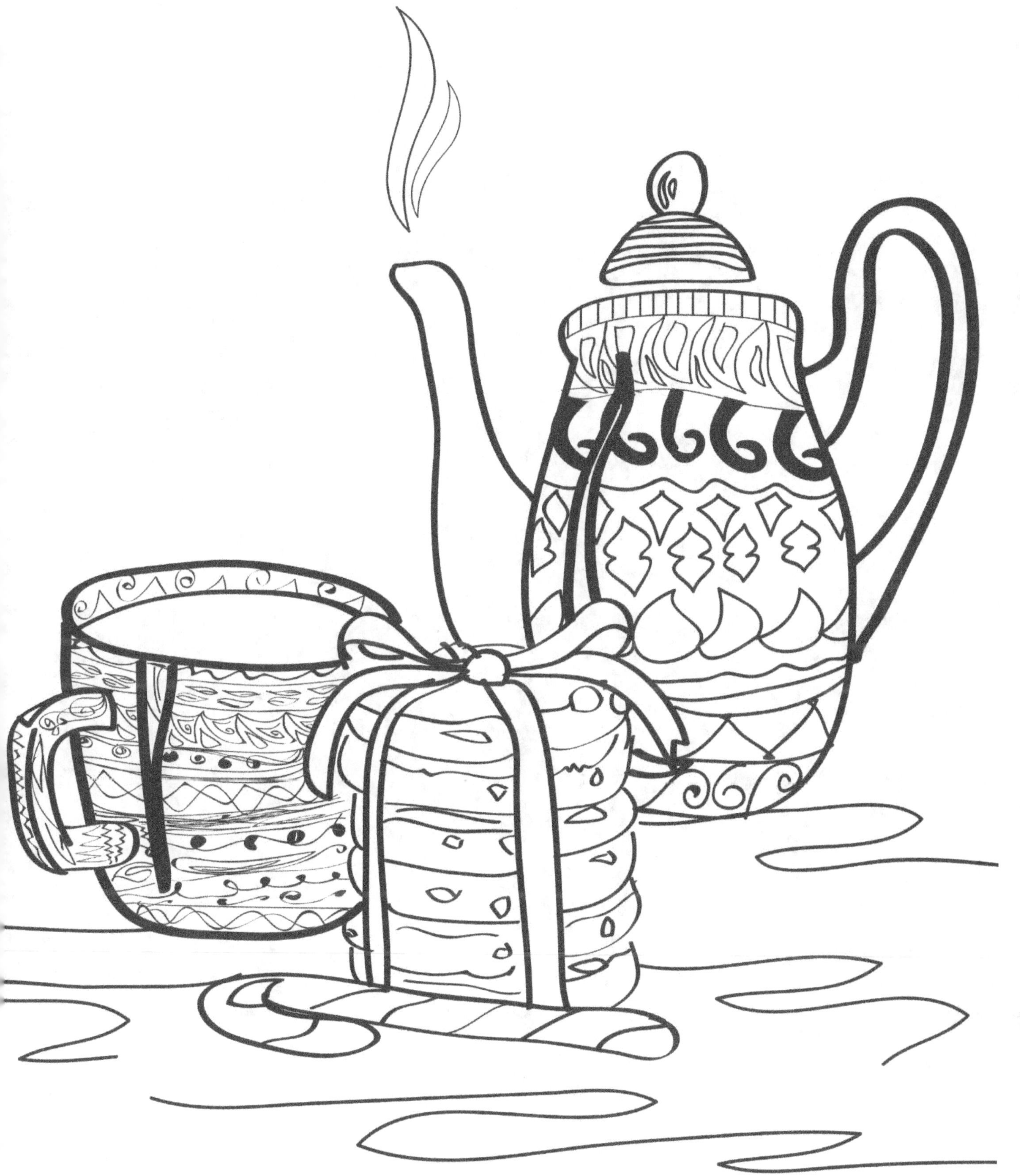

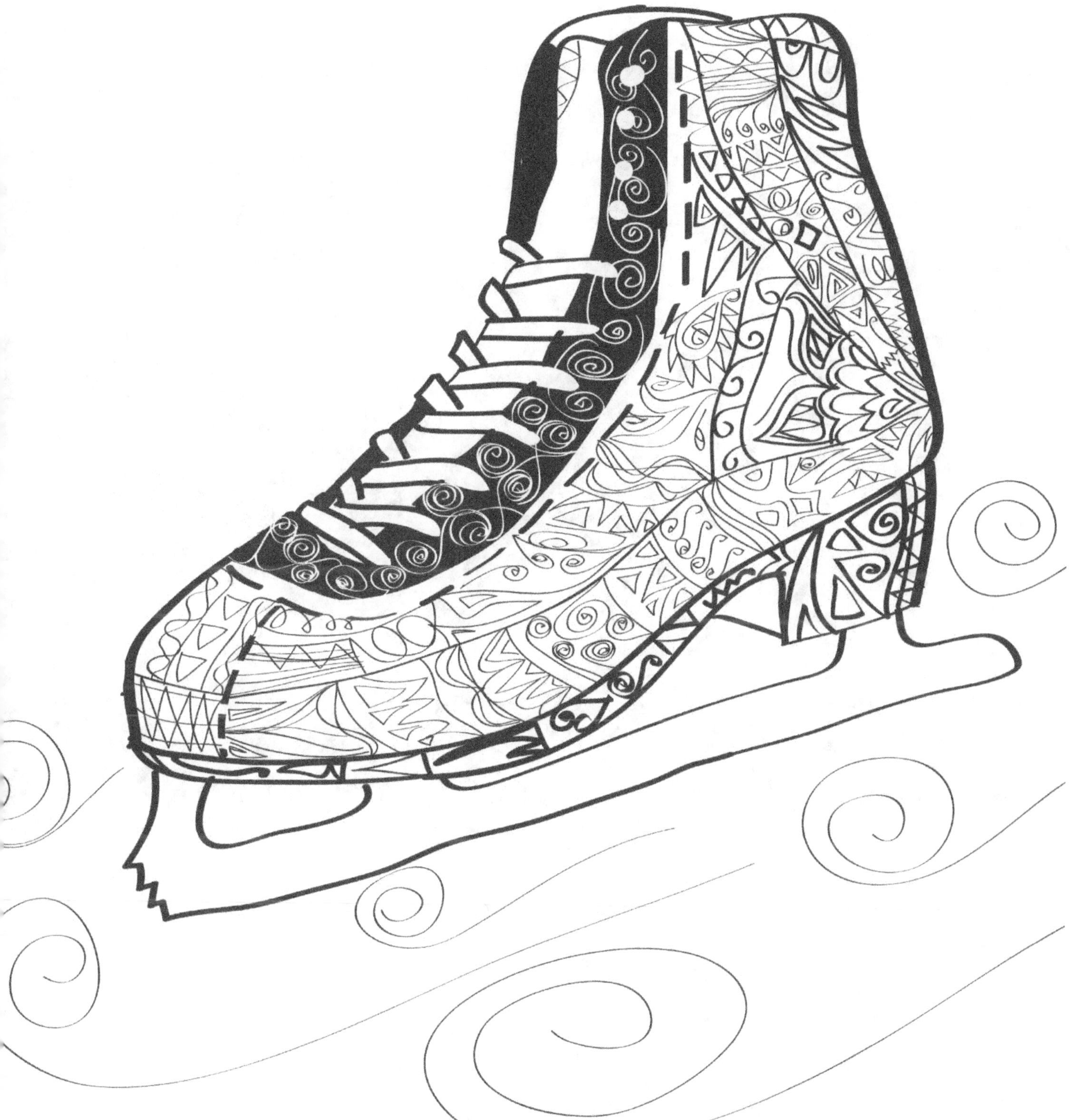

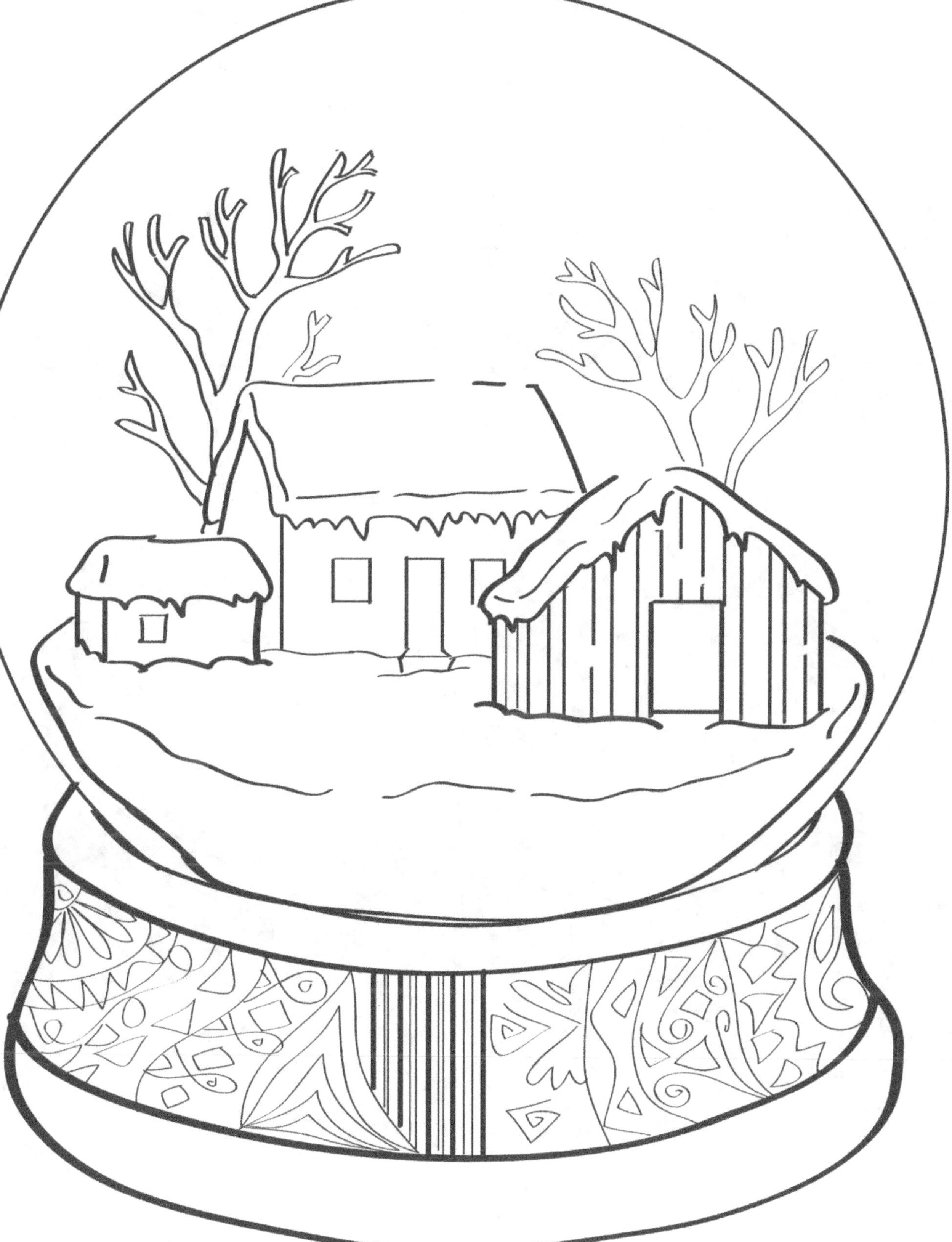

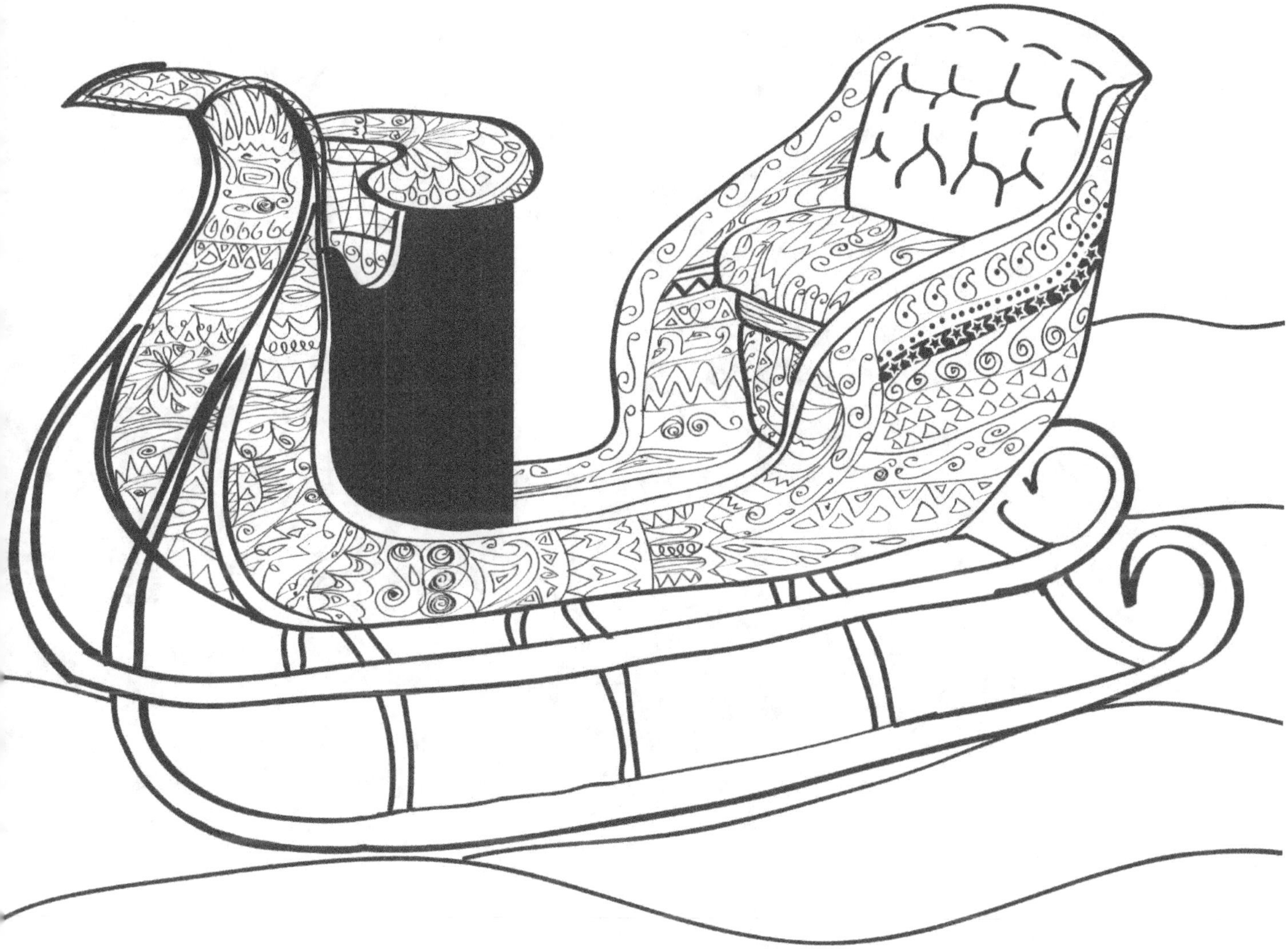

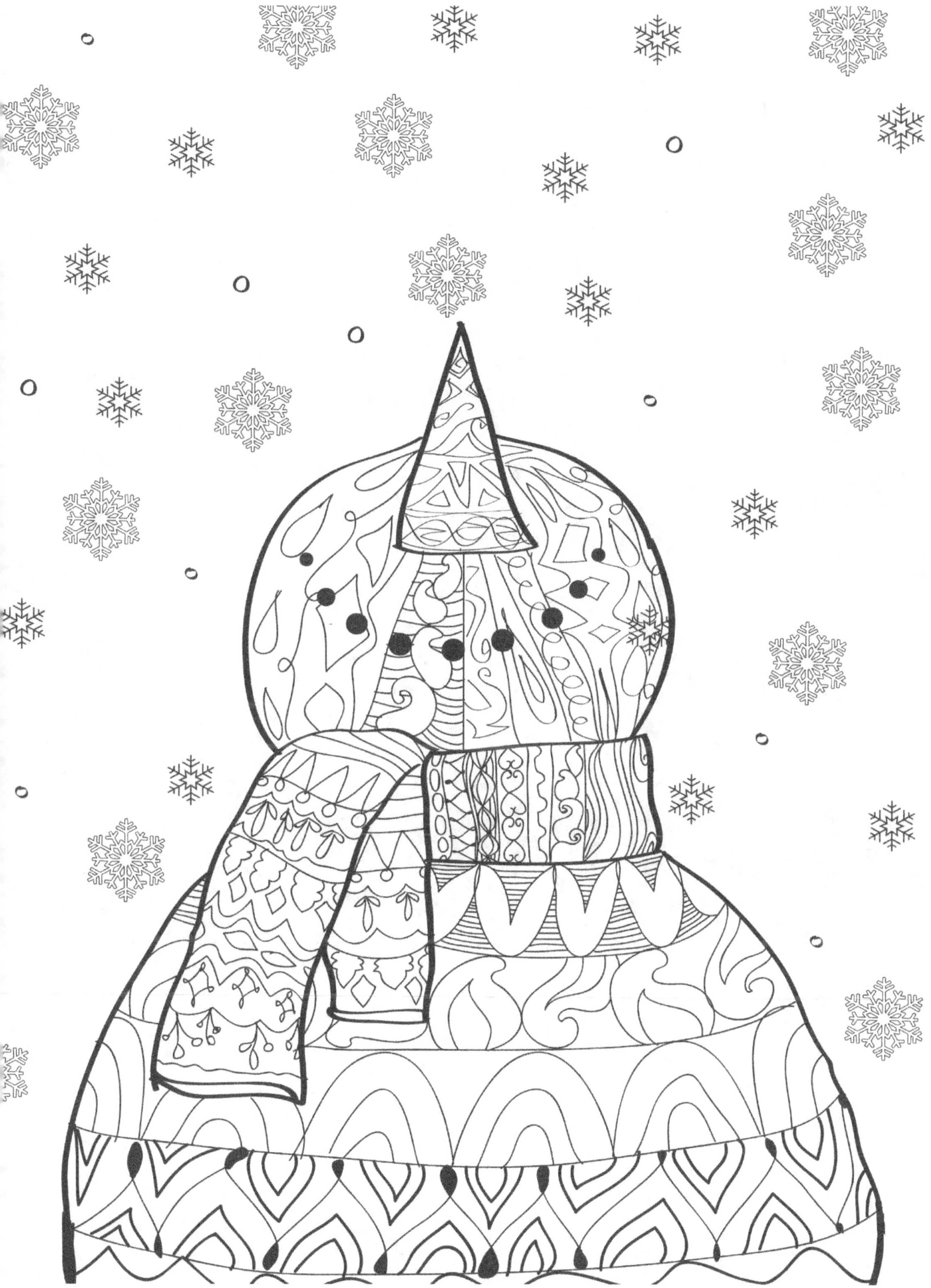

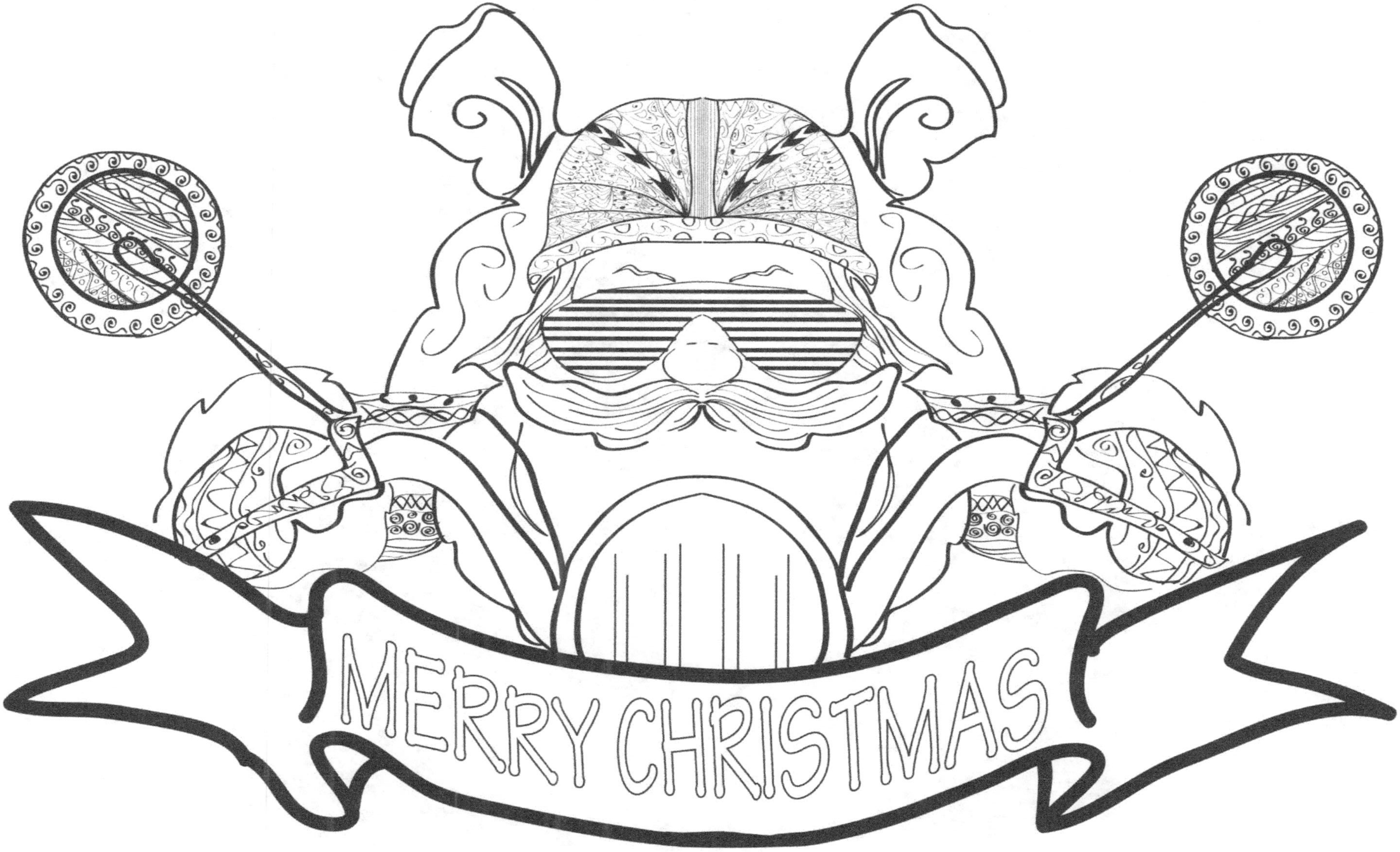
MERRY CHRISTMAS

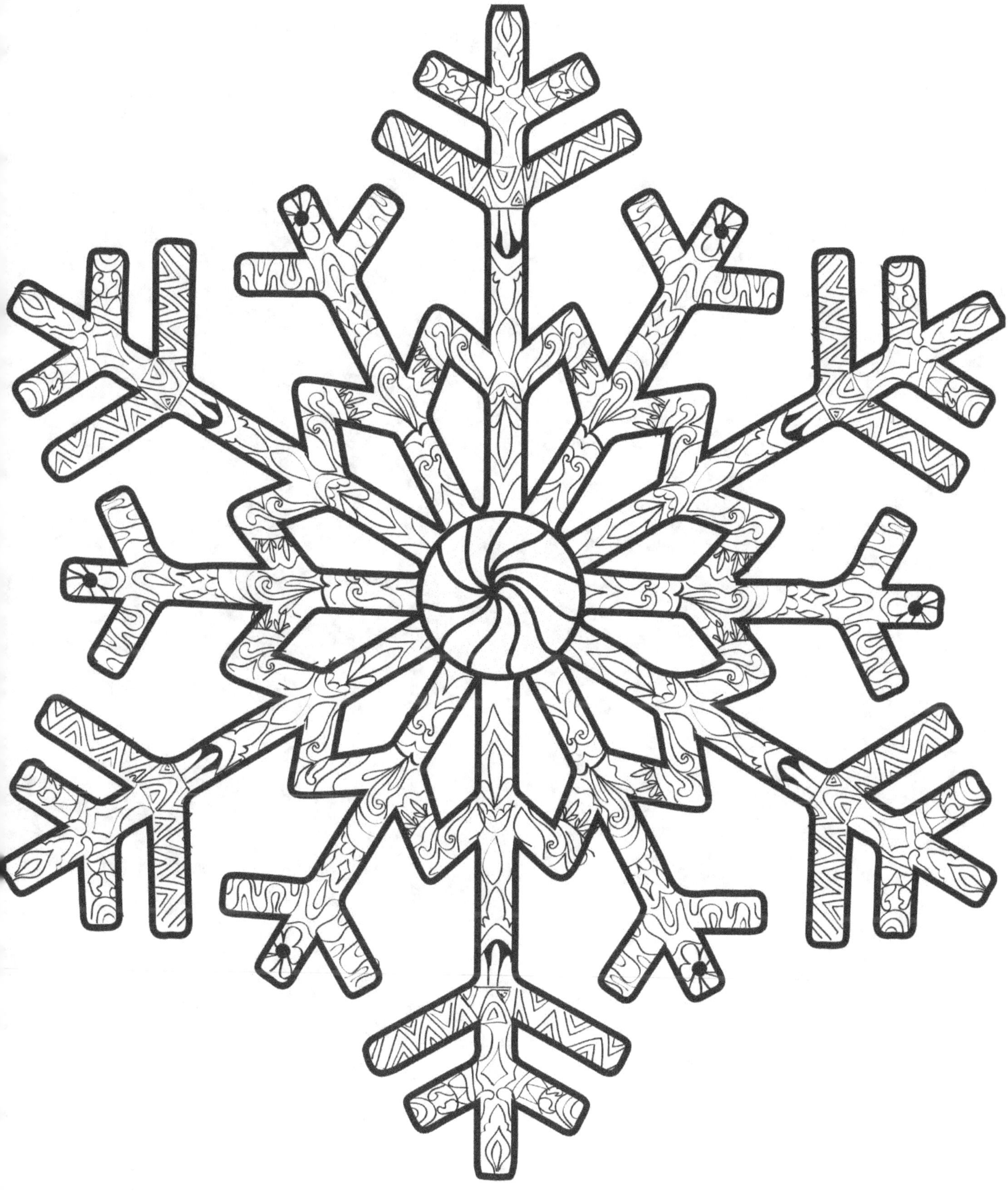

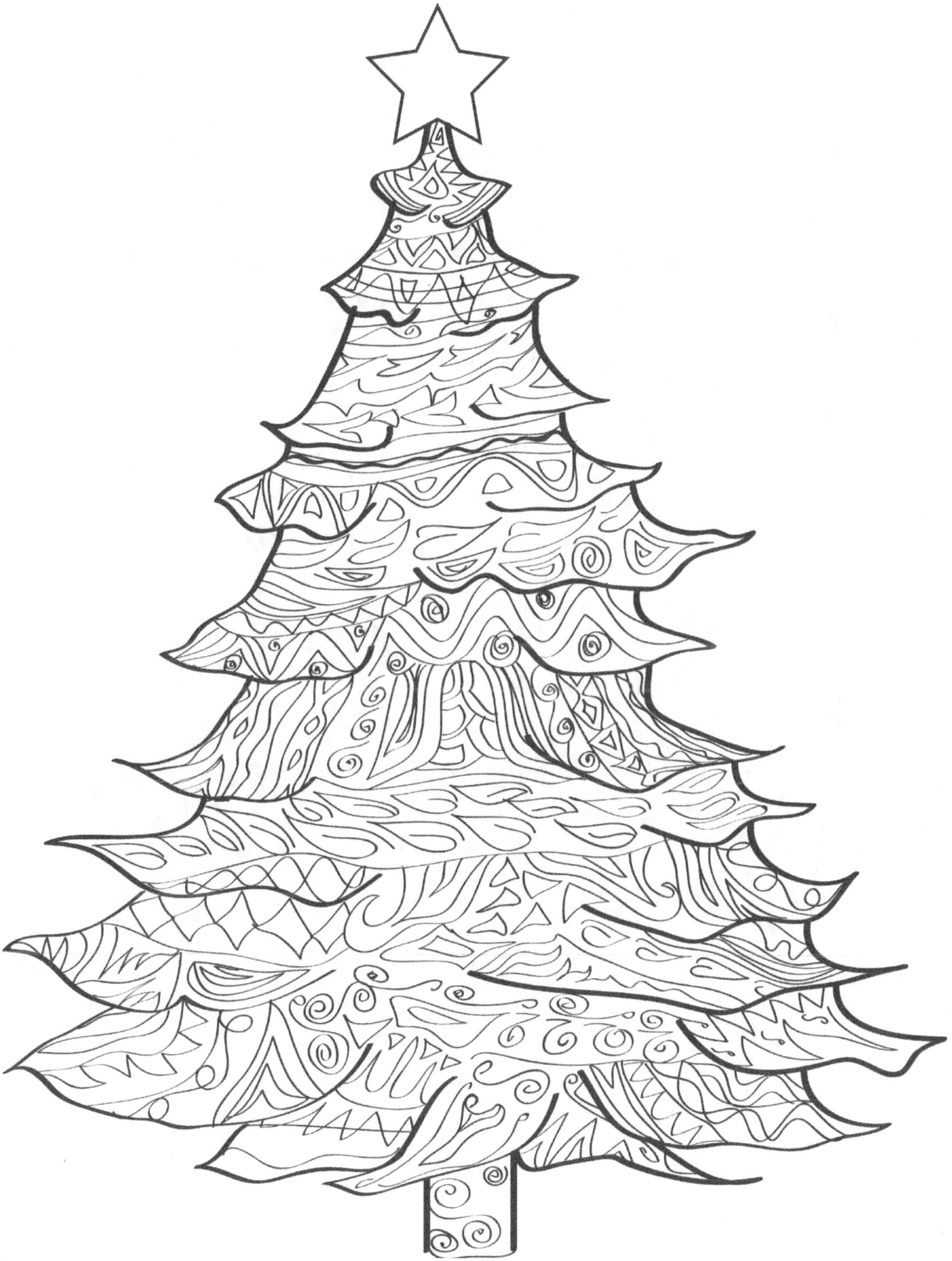

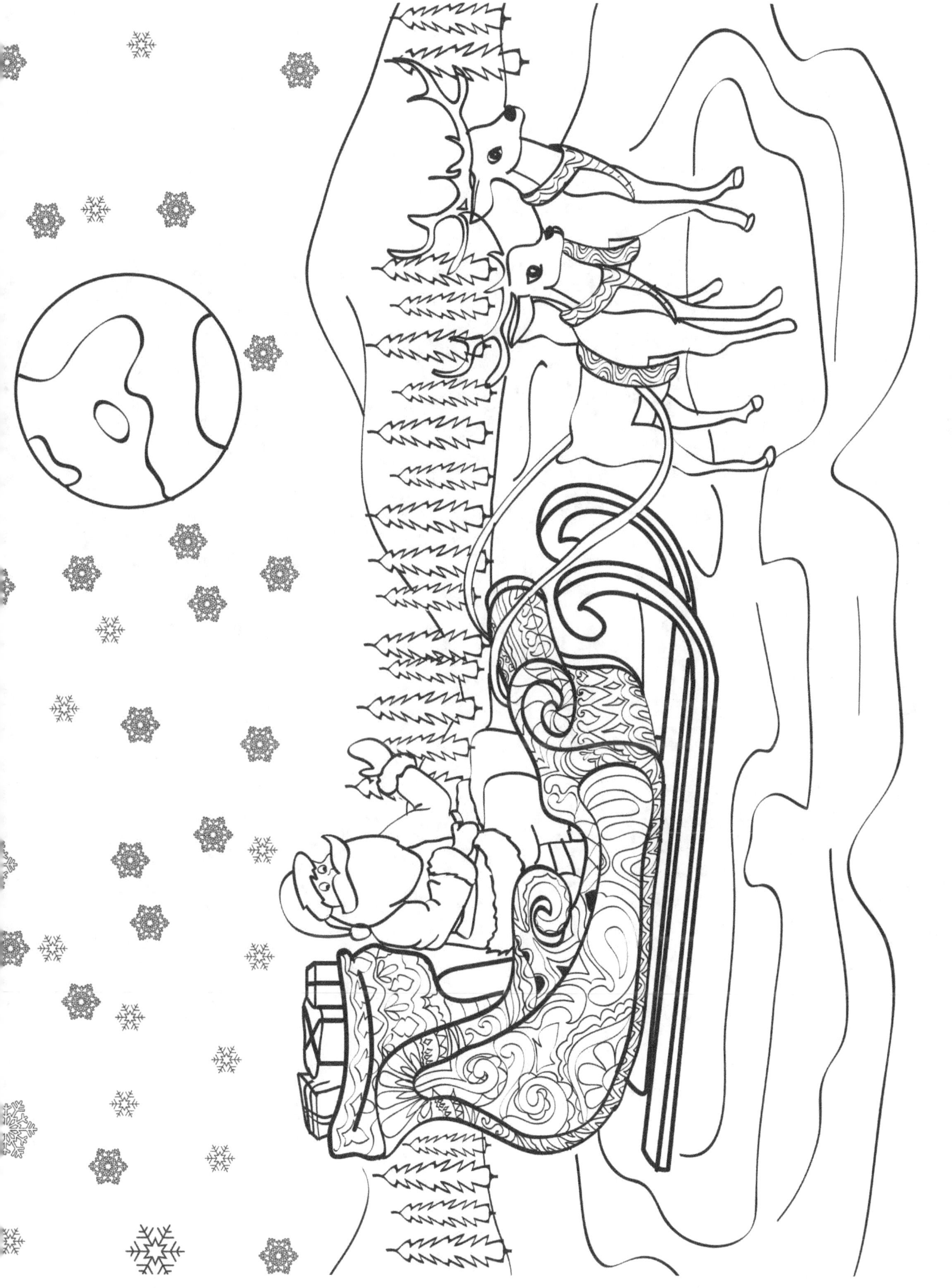

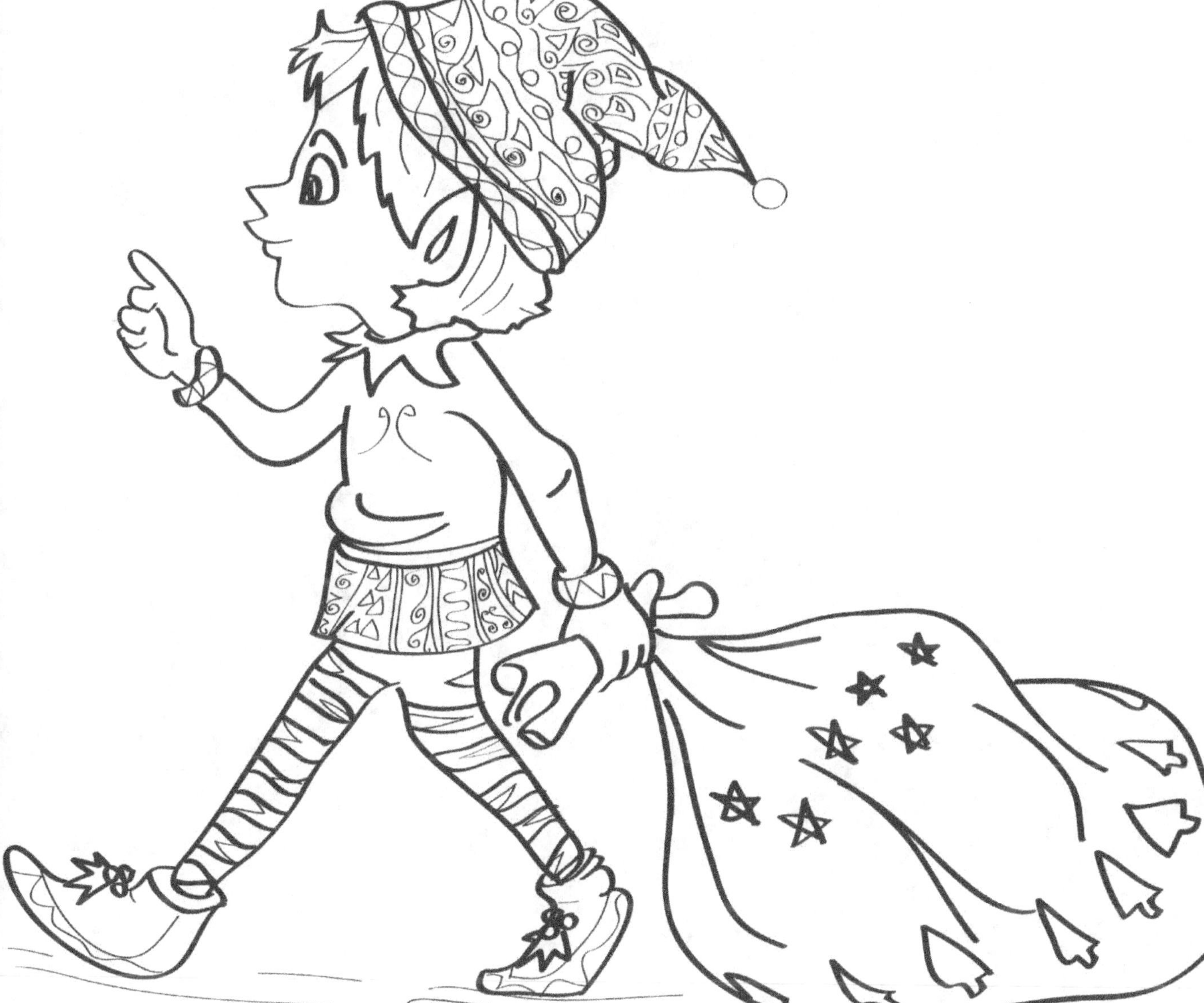

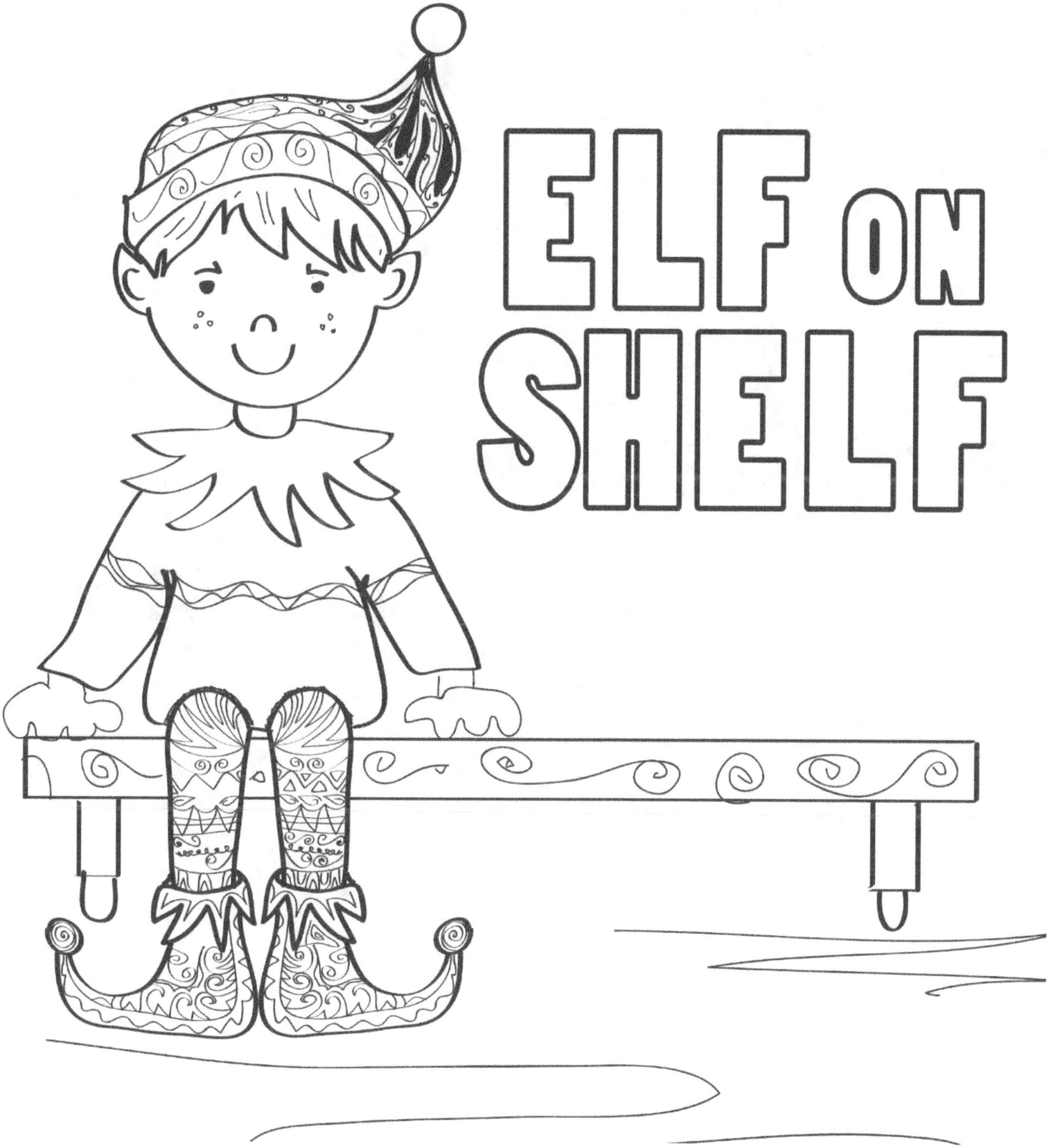
ELF ON
SHELF

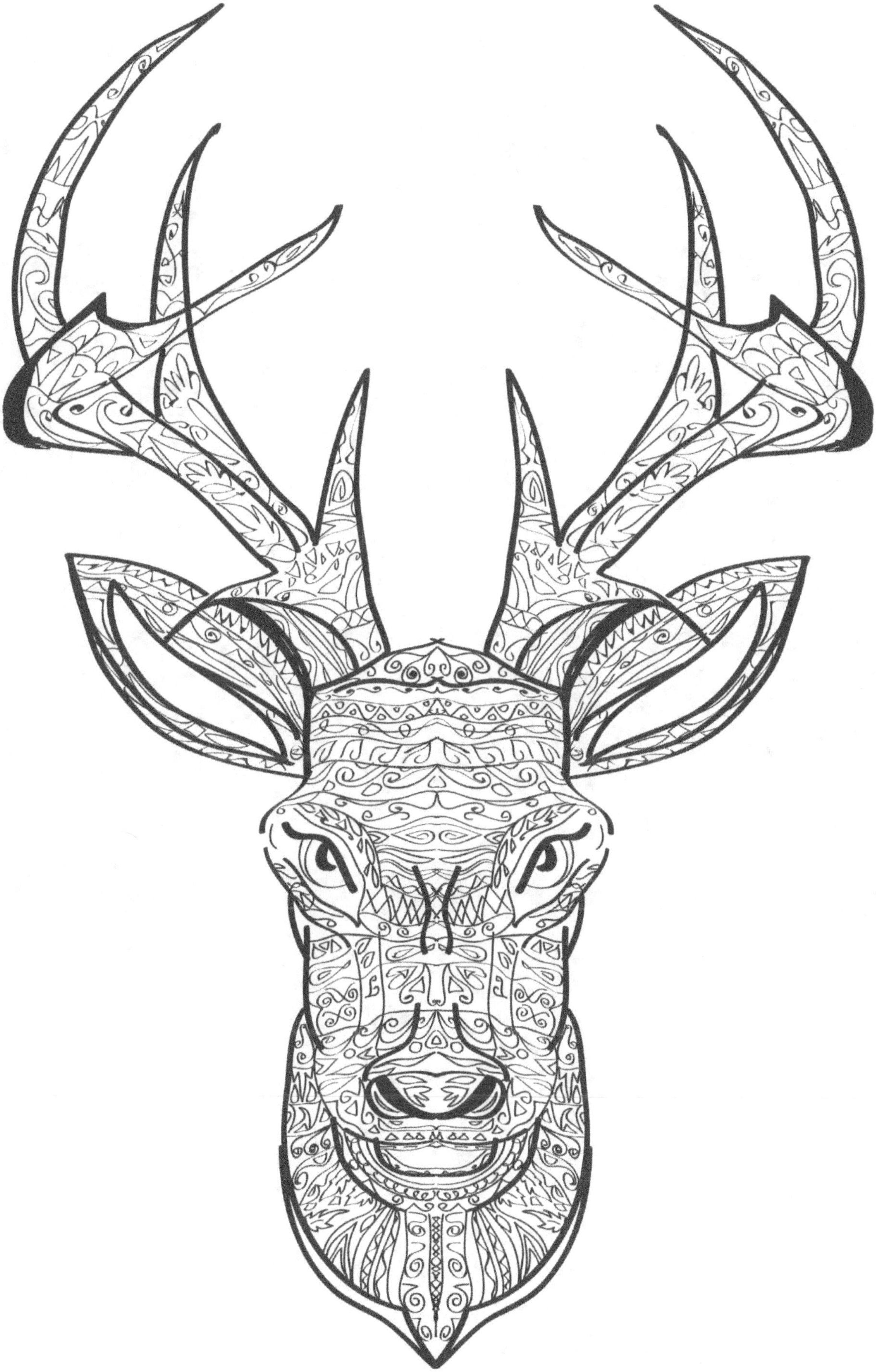

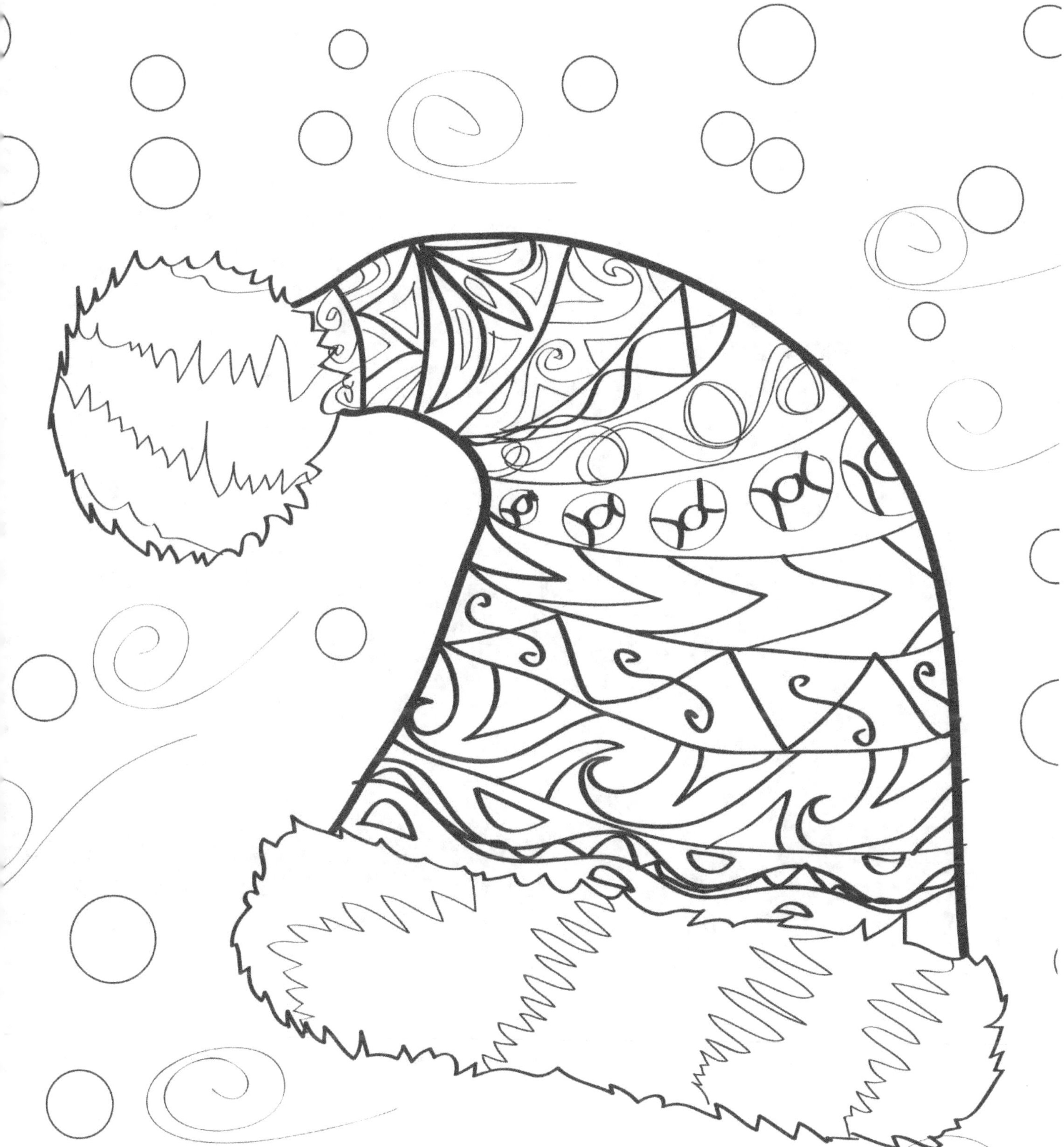

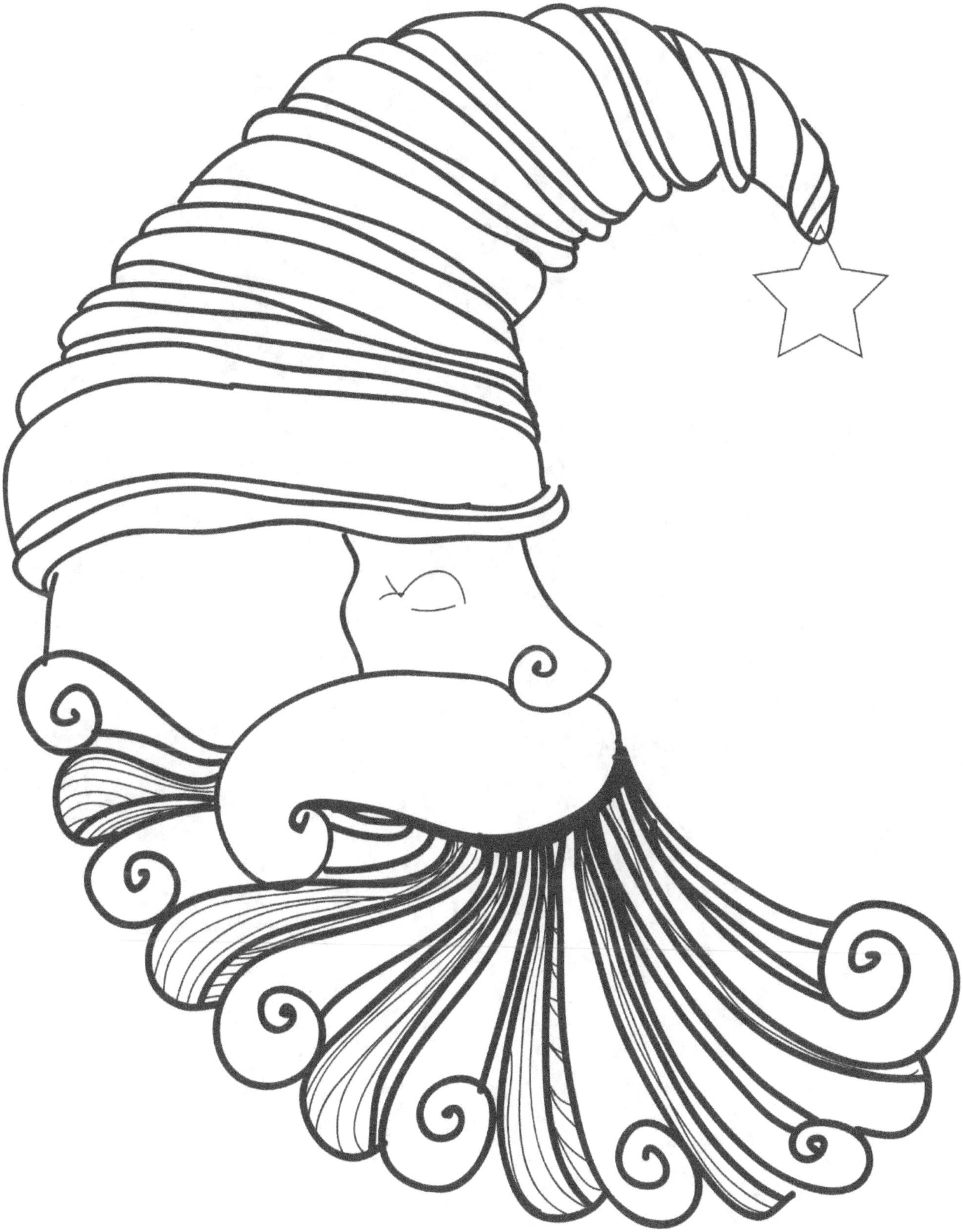

Other Coloring Books from Aryla Publishing

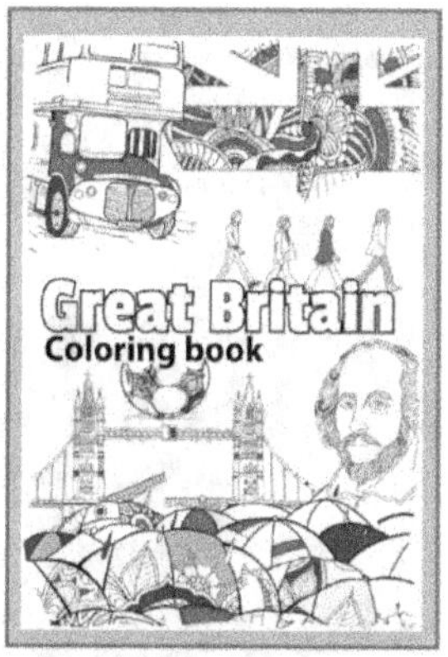

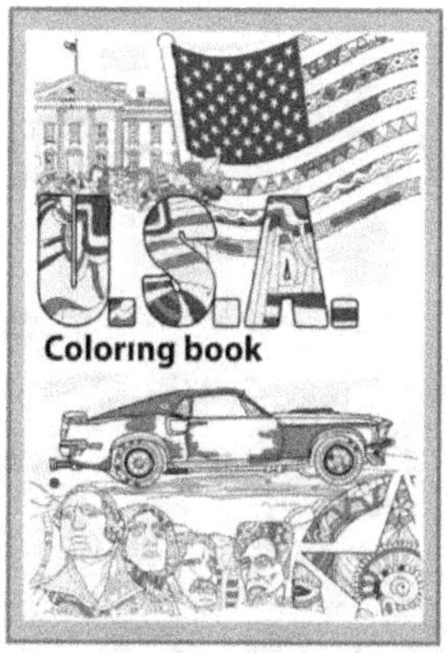

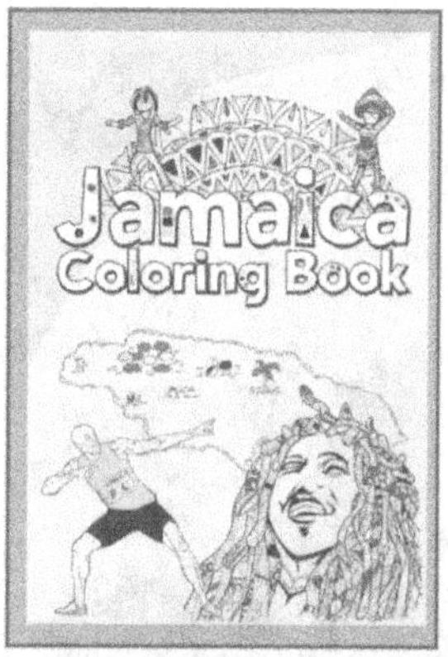

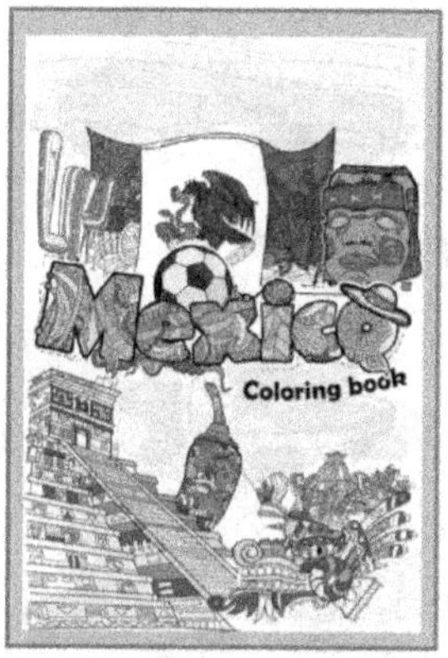

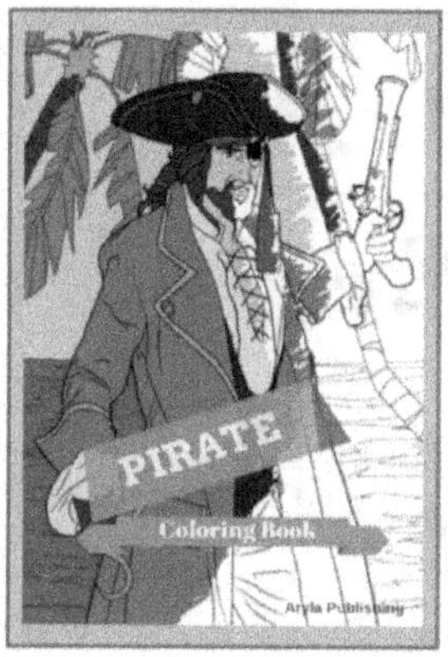

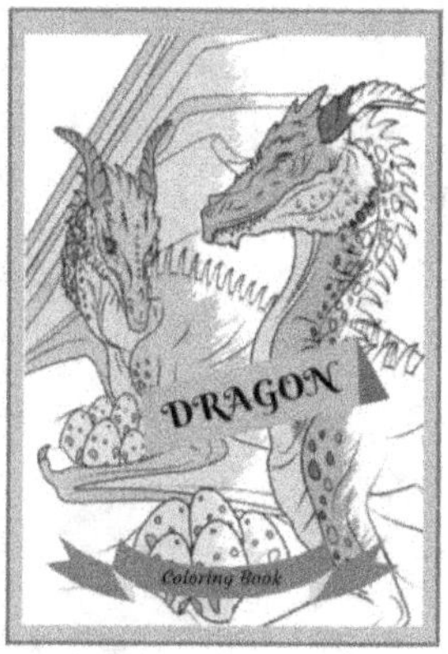

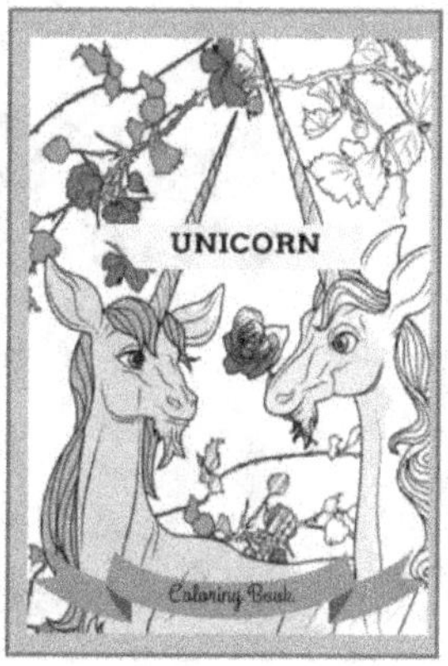

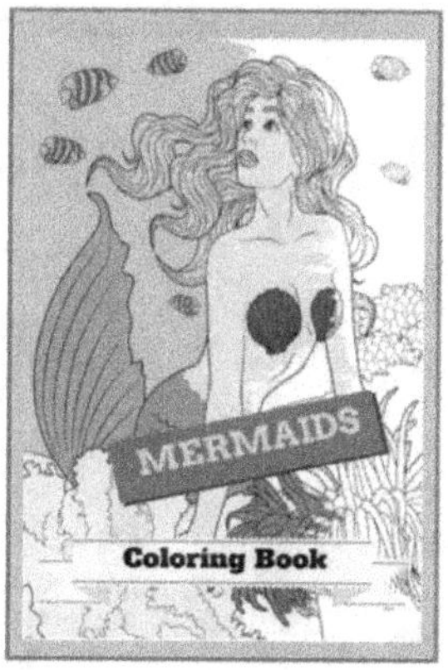

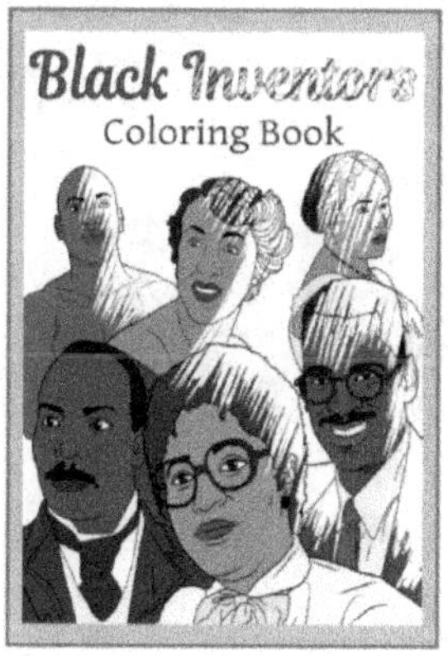

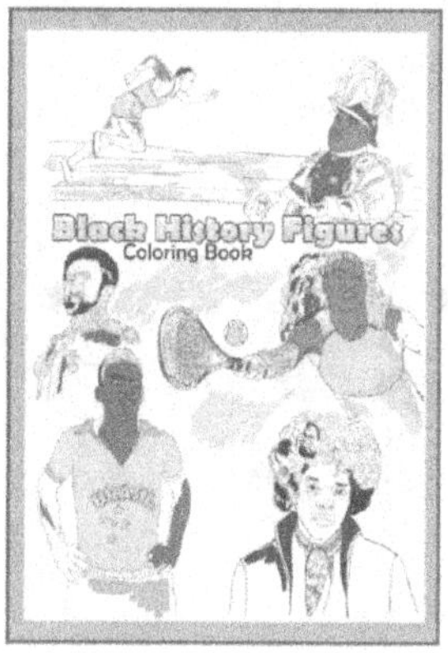

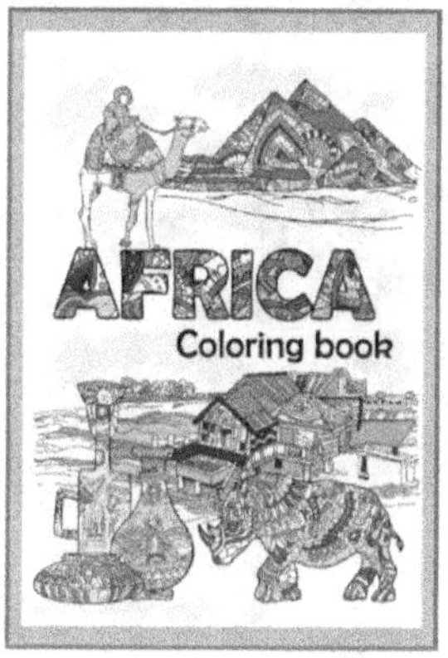

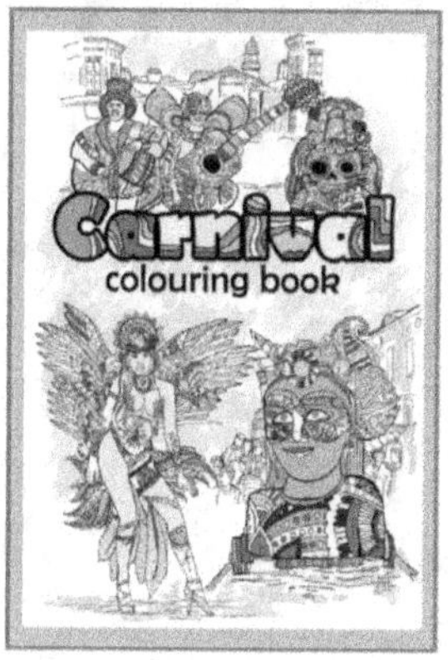

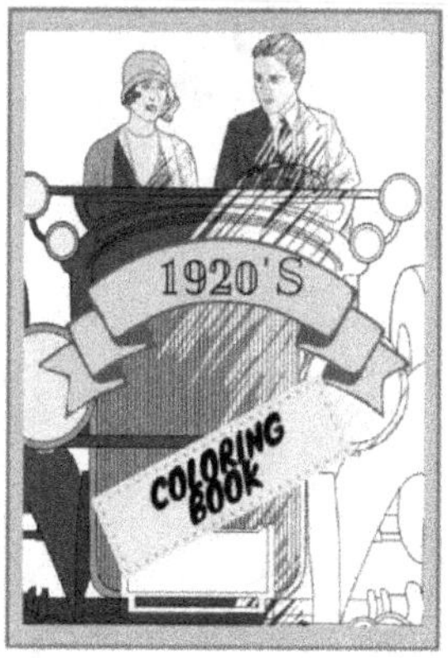

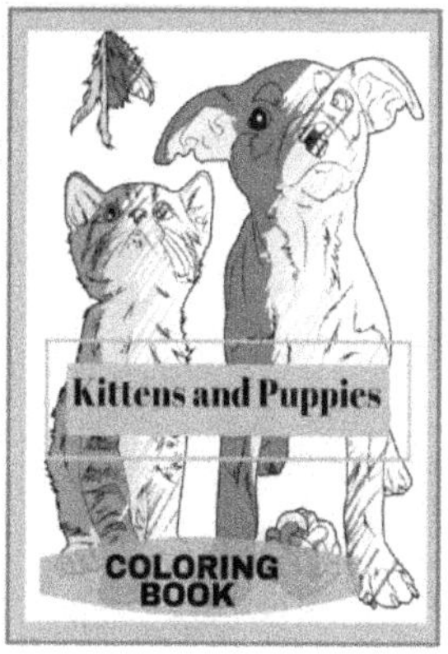

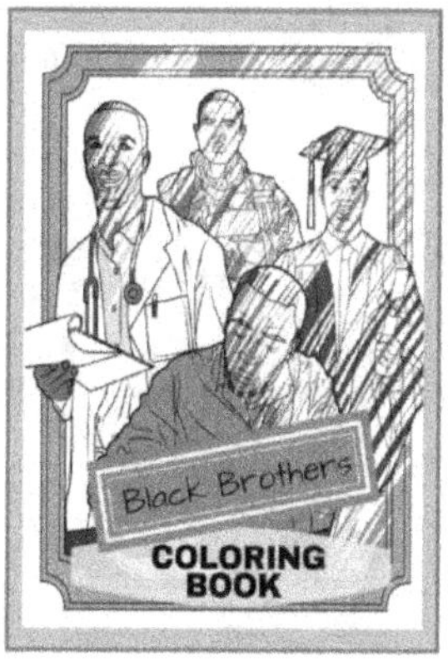

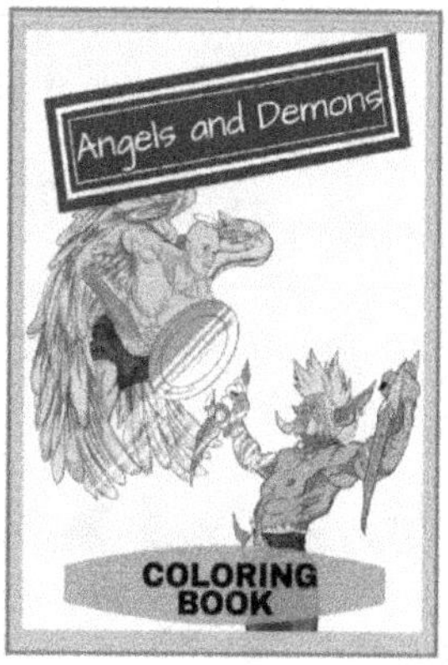

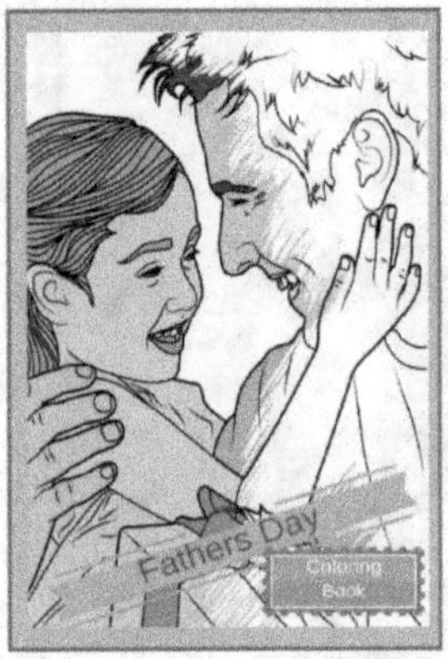
Fathers Day
Coloring Book
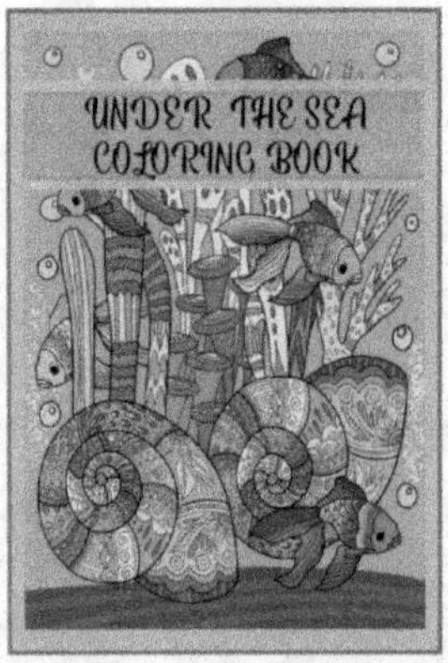
UNDER THE SEA
COLORING BOOK
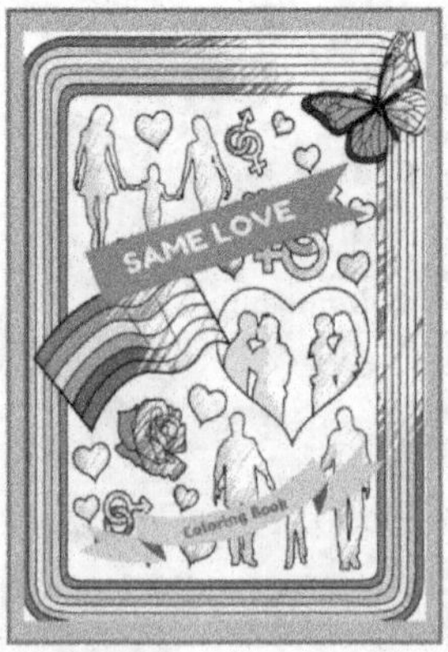
SAME LOVE
Coloring Book
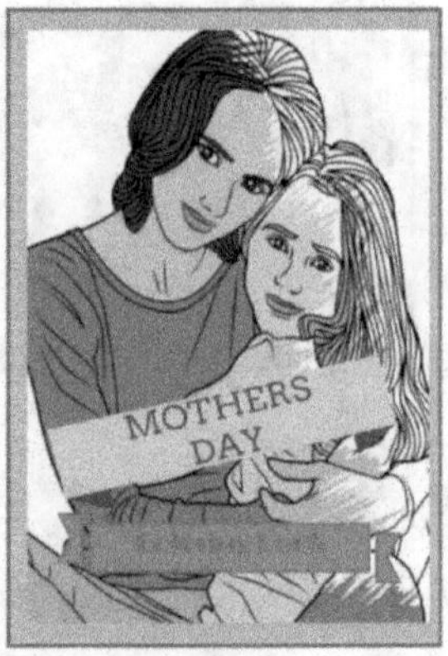
MOTHERS DAY
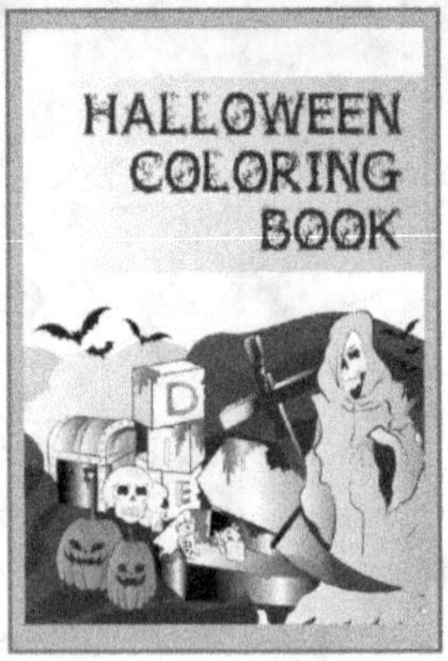
HALLOWEEN
COLORING
BOOK
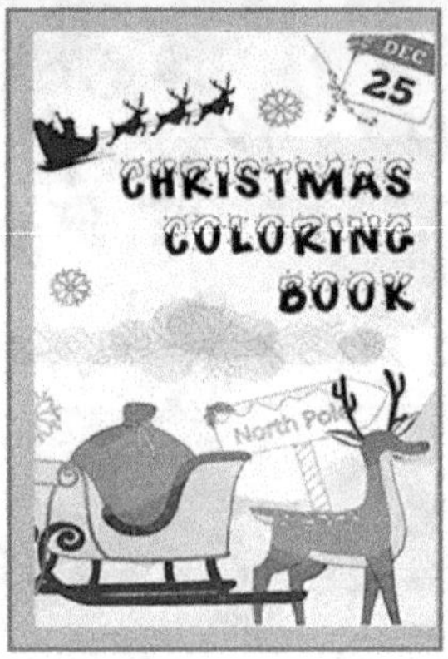
DEC
25
CHRISTMAS
COLORING
BOOK
North Pole
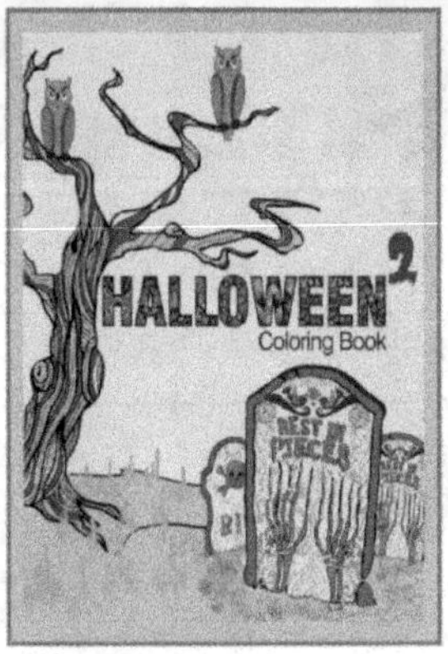
HALLOWEEN 2
Coloring Book
REST IN PIECES
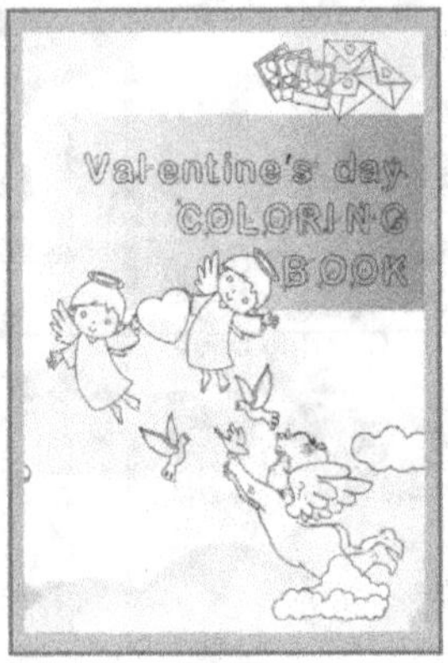
Valentine's day
COLORING
BOOK
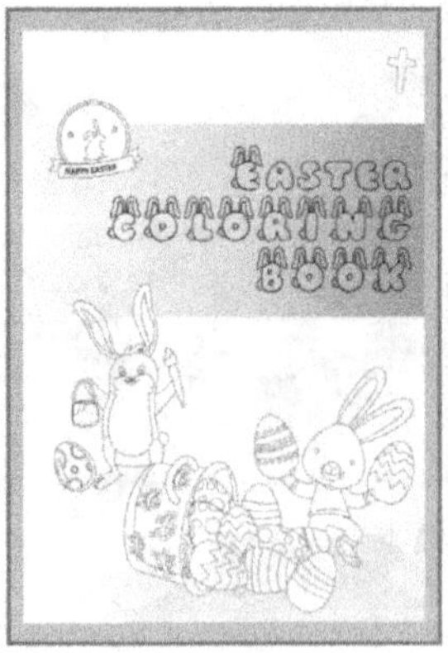
EASTER
COLORING
BOOK

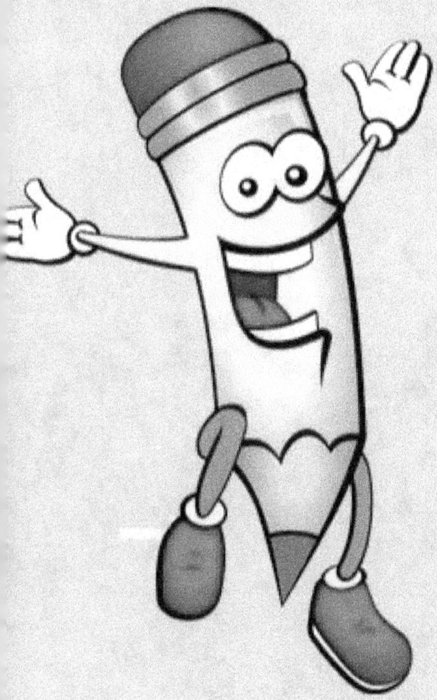

WE WOULD LOVE YOUR FEEDBACK

PLEASE LEAVE REVIEW AT:-

www.amazon.com/gp/product-review/1912675536

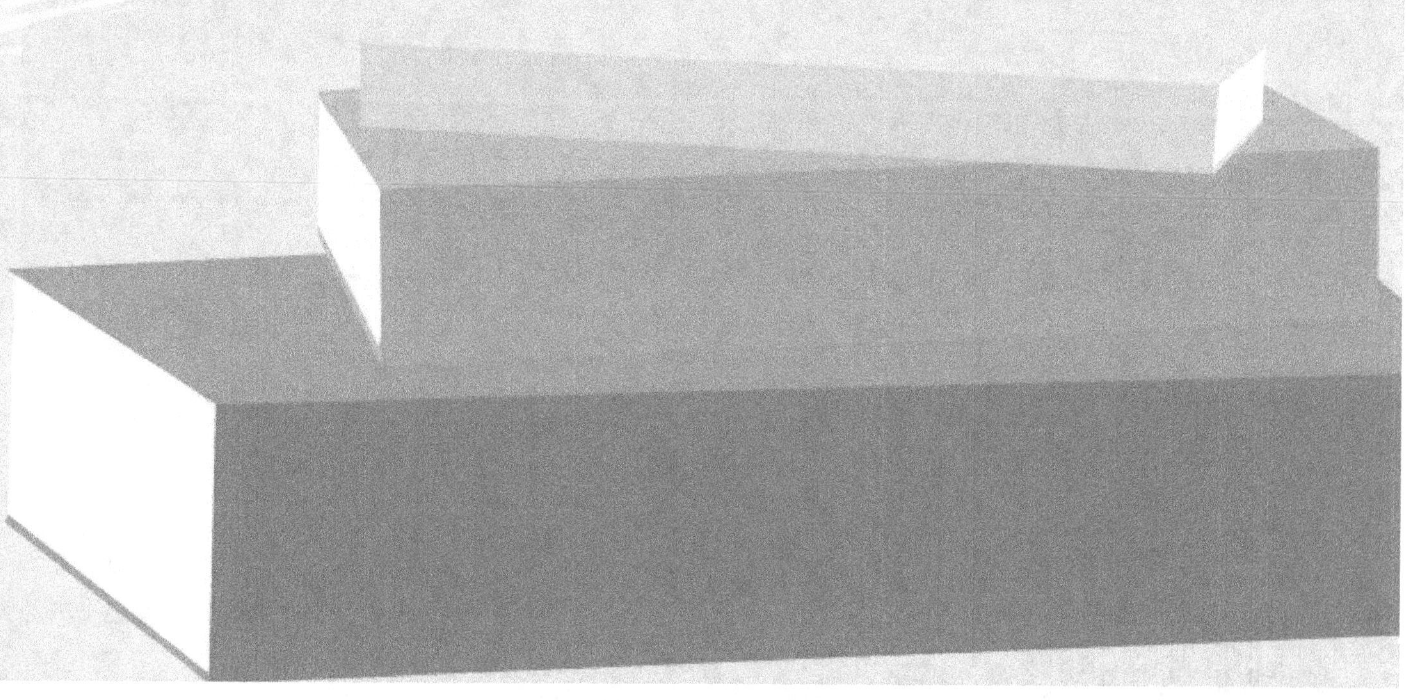

www.ingramcontent.com/pod-product-compliance
Lightning Source LLC
Chambersburg PA
CBHW081635220526
45468CB00009B/2444
* 9 7 8 1 9 1 2 6 7 5 5 5 5 *